GOD ANSWERED "EQUALITY"

By Betty C Dudney

Have an Awe of God, instead of just fear!

Once I went beyond my fear of God to discover Godly Peace. Then Joy filled my heart, my whole being! Do not delay coming back to God from Where we were given The Holy Gift of breath. Make the most of your life here on earth, for Eternal Rewards, here and there!

"You can still return to Me
       With all your heart" Joel 2:12

TO THOSE WHO LOVE GOD

OUR CREATOR, SPIRIT OF HOLY LOVE

EQUALLY FOR THOSE WHO HAVE YET TO KNOW

TO "LOVE ONE ANOTHER"

5

CONTENTS

INTRODUCTION

Almost fifty years after being given the Prophetic Word of "EQUALITY", have been witnessing to The Church to end their discrimination against the female half of God's Image. Without what only they can do end inequality within the largest of our Christian religions, how can we expect it to be ended anywhere else?

Found out half of all people in our world are trying to live on wages that average $3 a day! Not an hour, a day! One of our biggest problems with false beliefs of inequality alright, at least for others.

For some, Profit has become their God, or god. Resulting in less than 2% in control of 90% of our world's economy and much of our natural resources God meant for the benefit of all. Causing as many as 20,000 children to starve to death, yes, daily. Millions more including adults will go to bed hungry tonight.

Consider also as many of our young children in our world are unable to go to school, to learn to read or write, because they will have to work, as young as 5-6 years old!

"EQUALITY" IS God's Answer, our best answer for a good, free from wars world, a heard by many Prophetic Word meaning Equal Rights, Equal Respect, Equal Concern! The fullness of the Universal Golden Rule, to treat others as you would most want to be treated.

It does not mean everybody should have equal amounts of

anything, except for a Universal safety net for the poorest. So they too can know, life matters, even eternally our Spiritual moral life.

Are not People more important than profits? Should we not have honest fair wages for all people's labor, child raising, cooking, cleaning, if we want Peace, safety honestly from others?

Some protest "Equality" in terms of Equal Opportunity is not practical, or not from God. Yet Scriptural definitions tell us God is "not a god of partiality" *

*1 Duet.10:18; Acts 10:34; Romans 2:11. Only God worth our worship, one of Equal Justice, Holy Love, Equity. Over 500 Biblical verses relating to the non-partiality of God. For All, us sinners, as well as the Self-Righteous.

7

HUMMINGBIRDS AND GOD'S

One morning sitting behind the screen of my back door watching a few house sparrows eating breadcrumbs a tiny silver sliver of a Hummingbird noticed, and hovered in midair, less than a foot away from my face, it seemed to be saying thank you for feeding us, as it clicked, click, clicked away, then flew to a honeysuckle flower nearby.

Such little ones must see me like a big god, among others who could care less, just as I can only 'see' my God in a limited way.

All uniquely limited in what we see or perceive God to be! For a long time now, there have been few doubts for me, partly because of several supernatural experiences, such as seeing literally the Hand of God on my wall, so obviously beyond my daily reality, when I was only five years old, on my Birthday, no less, scared me from even trying to talk to God until my brother and I were decided to get Baptized at 14, he was a little over 12.

It would be twenty-five years later, in my middle thirties, before God would give me another such supernatural sign, and only then, when I was freely willing, to allow God's Holy Spirit fully into my heart, mind, and soul. "Rebirth" Jesus called it, from what He said in John 3:3-8. Only then could I or would I really get to know God's Holy Spirit, who wanted to help guide me, because like all of us with free will prefer to use our own, what I know now was a lesser will, because it unfairly mostly concerned just me, not equally others or our world too. A lesser selfish kind of Love. Not very Godly, that eventually causes us all kinds of worldly injustice to others that comes back to us in many harmful and hurtful ways.

Ideas or thoughts from our own minds, or other God Created beings, should first be tested or confirmed by The Golden Rule found naturally in good loving hearts, not damaged or hurt too much, that advices to treat others equally fair, as you would most want to be treated, even to your enemies Jesus also said. "This is the Laws and Prophets to put God first and Love One Another". *2 Matthew 5:44; 7:12; 22:39-40; Luke 6:27.

Moses saw God's Hand 4000 years ago, while given the Ten Commandments. A couple thousand years later the prophet Daniel interpreted God's Finger writing on the wall of the King's Banquet Hall and seen also by many who were dining with Him. Over 200 times, I have found the mention of God's Hand in our Scriptures, usually a symbolic sign of God acting in the world. Sometimes, literally seen.

The Universal Golden Rule of treating others with equal fairness, the way you would most like to be treated, is found in all our major world religions, as well as in the created hearts of most developed forms of human life. The doing of good, instead of evil, even to our enemies, makes it possible to create friendships, to lesson tensions and misunderstandings, at least not increase feelings of resentments, revenge.

Yet some are born emotionally hurt, damaged, or deficient, or can later be brain damaged, especially in the higher more sensitive areas of the human brain, resulting in the lack of their ability to feel for, or care about others, except as it affects their own immediate self. They would notice this, maybe be aware early in life of their lack of positive or good feelings for others

12

and would tend to hide that lack of caring. We don't seem to be very good at being Godly, what we were Created to be and is our nature, until you believe with all your heart, mind, Spirit, by the experience or real belief in a Loving, more Intelligent, Creative God. Maybe only then does God give your Spirit a Soul! Only God Knows for sure. Jesus spoke much of what we call in English 'Hell'. In original Hebrew, and the Aramaic language people of those days 2000 years ago spoke, it meant the loss of life in the Holy Heavenly City of Jerusalem, of being thrown outside into the dump outside, where the fires constantly burnt, the waste to dust again.

Without the ability to feel or care for others, somewhat as equals, it is normal for one to use cunning, sneaky, even cruel ways to gain positions of power over others, just to get their own way, in the home, at work. For most dictators it has been in political, religious or economic positions, because of belief and former mostly men in power and the practice of inequality! Pleasure would come then, only by being in control, even to the misuse of others, for more important to them, selfish needs.

It is obvious to many, that our world has experienced several such persons in great power for the past five or more thousands of years!

Was not sure why we were going into our present Biblical like Plague until I began to remember my first conscious contact with God, at only five years old, the same month and year Hitler took control of country of Germany on the other side of my then world. Would learn little of the details for many years, even though one of my favorite Uncles, going to college near where we lived, signed up for the Air Force, almost as soon as he heard about the war to defend our Freedoms, here in America. My Dad had been a Marine for two years before his marriage to Mom, a country-school teacher, and later they would drive across this great land from upper Middle Tennessee with my uncle, to Compton in California, where there were good paying jobs in the nearby Oil fields, and where my Uncle Dawson, could go to college.

Within a few months this fun-loving Uncle, would join the Air Force and fly over 50 missions, a bombardier over Germany, and Italy. Shot down twice behind enemy lines, he came back physically unhurt, but using alcohol to deaden the mental anguish, pain of what he had had to see, do, experience. The War without for him and millions of soldiers there and here, became a personal spiritual war within. 5000 years of wars!

In the middle of this Biblical Plague of inequality, it is not just to be blamed on one such evil leader, when many of those over us, support taking away people's Freedoms for their own selfishness, as well as our own lack of knowledge, sometimes concern or priority of doing what each of us can do to stop it, like vote, standing up for equal rights that stop only at the equal rights of others.

Till then we remain in great danger of World War III, this time much worse, because it will be nuclear, enough to send us back to underground cities, already built by many governments!

The only good news in terms of war is we still have a choice we make daily with our God given free will. Those who still allow only God to have shared control.

We are not yet at the very end of "Revelation's end times", for past 2000 years, for more has yet to happen, some of it not even been started. More about that later.

We could with God's Help, choose to go towards a "1000 years of Peace" instead! Most people don't even seem to know that. But it is the main reason Prophecy is given to us at all. Till the Messiah or Christ does come or return, there will be time to prevent even a nuclear war, if you confirm with God if don't believe me, for a negative voice will try to tell you that you are powerless.

I have had three Extra-Ordinary Spiritual Contacts with God's Holy Spirit over the past 70 years that tells me differently, but not unless and until most or enough are willing to come out of the sin of inequality!

All limited to some degree, in our feelings for those we don't see much like us, those of a different race or sex, not culturally, raised in a similar way. Yet we are all on an evolving path, on our way to a higher spiritual perfection, that's why we have been given life here and now, if when we so choose.
Much of our learning has been on a cultural level as well as on an instinctive level, only very gradually have we increased in conscious awareness of what can be. This could help explain the last many years of our patriarchal oppression, enforced by those in the very top positions of the majority in Political, Economic, Religious powers. Leading us into One after another War mostly for the 1%'s profit.
Our history is full of such Cesar's, Kings, even a few Queens, who have had little conscience in using or misusing people, or how they increase their own power, gain or fortune.
Wars are against the best and highest interest for most, actually all people, instead of our seeking cooperation, negotiating solution's, what the female half more naturally excels at.

Where the more aggressive males lack and often fail because of having more male aggressive hormones, that can cause much emotional, spiritual and often eventually physical destruction, if not treated physically and/or spiritually.

We can only expect this to continue, until we are able to insure more legal, as well as other kinds of cultural safeguards of "Equality", for People's Equal Rights. So not as easy to misuse positions of power as it is now.
Democracy, so Precious, is not worth giving the people's power over to a Dictator, or King who wants to take your best.

Most of us need such safeguards, with many reasons to fear those who are controlled by evil desires or plans who want to also keep us in wage slavery, while they reap even up to 90% or more Profits!
Have seen many examples of how it is possible when just a few, who have had enough, commit to coming together. Just the simple beating of pots and pans once with spoons, with some walking through neighborhood streets, when only a few rallied hundreds of people eventually who spoke up in a local community meeting with the governing leaders, for their needs that worked! What does it take for the many worldwide needs? Easy to feel overwhelmed to even start but we have few alternatives, with the desperate lives of so many needs most of our world faces?
Those who are in power are not going to get better, until we are willing to recognize what is, deal with it best we can. If we do know something better for all and choose to leave undone, then we may, or not be able to say, as many said after World War II:

"When they finally came into my neighborhood, I was still afraid but could no longer do anything".

fear of lesser gods, we have allowed to guide, instead of God's Holy Spirit in our heart, is our worse enemy! God warned the Israelites from the beginning, of scriptures, when they wanted to have a King, like other nations. Telling them to have such rulers, instead of the Judges they did have, would cost them much and look how much it has cost them?

History tells us Dictatorships are seldom good for most of the people. Wars killing off the young, doing untold damage to the minds left on both sides, as well as taking often personal and needed resources, even people's daily control, except for the most privileged.

Political leaders, even some Religious, are into the sin and idolatry of male/only control and not Equally Loving of the people of different races or culture.

Believing in the right of the male nature to rule over the other half of their Godly Nature, the female half, partly from misinterpretation of Scriptures, written and slanted towards the male half!

"Equality" is the only Word of Prophecy for our times, God has given me to share. By telling you unless you have quit caring it now becomes your responsibility too to confirm for yourself or suffer possible eternal damage to your soul, if you now have one? Unless you have a good excuse why not?

It is not a good idea anyway, to let anyone rule over your Soul, but a Loving "ABBA", Your Heavenly Parent, as Jesus confirms and the Word Jesus used for God. As well as the first Commandment given to Moses. No idolatry, it leads to repeating the past, with even worse disasters, now such as nuclear wars, affecting many for hundreds, even thousands of years. Most likely has in the world's History, as increasingly more evidence in Archeological is now showing us.

Prophets have been warning of a World War III for a long time, we have so far barely managed to avoid, more than a few times. It is going to take many of us living, to be able to prevent the worse now from happening.

To warn us of the danger we are in, is one of the main reasons Prophecy is given. God does not want to end our Free Will. Has in the past, like in this present Biblical like Covid Plague that forces us to make changes, to pause and reexamine the way we are choosing to live. Free will choices each of us do make, as the ones being here at this time and place and will be held, in some ways equally responsible for what we do, or fail to do, those now forewarned! Be thankful for having such a warning, ignore at your own peril!

The only sensible way, is to start first with yourself, asking only a Loving God into a cleaned, forgiven heart, so you can hear, be able to know best, what best to do. Only a Loving heart working together with a Godly Intelligence, inner and outer, is going to be able to 'See', know more than our limited physical minds and hearts, in this limited space and time can know!

To be able to be guided to the "Fullness of Truth", such as in John 3:3 and John 14:26, Jesus promised those willing to repent of past sins, ask forgiveness where possible, even for those who have hurt you.

God will forgive you if sincere, you cannot fool God! Give you the Grace to Love such a God, as well as One Another.

We face besides wars, many social dangers such as the rise of GMOs, as the present DNA changing of our Food Seeds, by making even God given Organic food seeds sterile, when grown near the now many owned or leased, commercial GMO's farms, formerly individual family farms, many taken over by higher cost of people's needs, in just living.

Remember that small groups of like-minded friends working with each other for a better world, have made a difference many times and can do so again. Plenty on this earth for all to have, enough food, housing, education, but limited only when we allow such a few greedy, selfish, amoral men to control up to 80 % of our world's economy and resources. Can you believe this? If not check for yourself.
It has been the strong-arming, the fear of loss of income, even sometimes physical violence that has been those in control ways of controlling, using fear to scare away the need of oversight, to be able to take advantage, to have control can become addictive. To avoid falling into that kind of mindset, to actually turn the current control, must be done through legal means, Non-Violent Efforts, to avoid falling into the same amoral inequality.

Each of us can join others, to create networks with those you know, trust, to be interested in a better life, for themselves and equally for all.
Expect opposition, for the struggle is really for your Soul, as well as for the physical control! Having morals against the hurting of others for some is considered a weakness, those who are most greedy and self-centered. The human spirit, and/or our souls, would be in grave danger, if we knowingly supported inequality that now keeps up to half of the world's population on

a near starvation diet, and for so many other injustices.

To stop such inequality, many years ago, I felt led to witness to Pope Benedict XVI, after he became Pope, after many earlier attempts to witness to Pope John Paul II. Going to Rome the first time in1985, with the hope to help end much discrimination first within The Church, as one of the major places where our world's morality flows from!
To end discrimination against Racism and Sexism first, same as already given by God's Holy Spirit to the Bishops at Vatican II in 1965. Has been called within The Church about every 100 years for The World's Bishops to ask the Guidance of God's Holy Spirit. It would be ten years later before I would first hear the actual word of "Equality", during my own Spiritual Rebirth* * John 3:3.

In spite of God's message, most in control within The Church have ignored or make light of most of these discriminations against women especially since the death of Pope John Paul I, the first Pope elected after the Vatican council.
He had promised only a few days before, to over a hundred women religious who had come to the Vatican to ask him to end their discrimination, and it was also brought to his attention of the Vatican Bank irregularities. Only three days before his most sudden, untimely Death.
Now over 50 years later, we may have another such Holy Pope? He took the name of St. Francis. Pray that He is and for His personal protection!
Raised as a Protestant I had not even heard at that time of such a Catholic Council.

IDOLATRY

WE ARE TEMPTED TO MAKE GODS OUT FROM THINGS
IMPERFECT, ALLOWING EVIL, INEQUALITY TO
PROSPER WHILE THE YOUNG IN KNOWLEDGE SUFFER
THE MOST!

WHEN GOD ANSWERED "EQUALITY"

THEN DID MANY BEGAN TO COMMIT TO DAILY
FOLLOW A MORE PERFECT HOLY LOVE WITH ALL
OUR HEART, MIND, AND SOUL.

ONLY THEN CAN WE EXPECT TO HAVE THE BEST
POSSILBE GUIDANCE NOT BE CONTROLLED OR LED
BY FALSE GOD'S OF IDOLATRY, INEQUALITY.

On November 12th, 2010 sent this letter:

Pope Benedict XVI,
Vatican City, Roma, Italia

Bon Journo Padre,

   Have known from the beginning it would be difficult to communicate with you. The reason the person who reads this letter should know I have, at least two good reasons to believe our Pope has read some of many sent letters.
So please, do not try to stop this one.

   Even if we are in conflict, Love, with Godly Purpose it is the primary reason to change things for the better, for all of us.
   Inequality hurts all. What we do here, or fail to do, affects us in the present, as well as the hereafter. Inequality is still hurting The Church and is negatively affecting our world.
   God has allowed "Equality" to flow first from The Church. *1 God is not just male, or only female, but a combination of both gender qualities. "In Christ, there is no male or female." *2

   Every human being, scientifically, mentally, and most importantly spiritually, is composed of both sexual components, only in degree. We are much more alike than we are different!

I do not want to come to Rome for anything but You're Blessing for the Order of Mary, Michael's, for a Golden Rule Family.

Time is of the essence, for Our Church, for our world. If you continue to refuse to give women the right to serve "In Christ" at the altar, on the grounds Jesus did not appoint any, then the same logic can be applied that neither were Italians, poles, or Germans, only Jews were appointed!

Then I must come to Rome fasting and praying for the female half of God's Image. In the name of Christ,

Betty C Dudney E.M.

*1 Pastoral Constitution Vatican II
*2 Apostle St. Paul in Galatians 3:28

24

WHY GO TO ROME?

I came here to help, with the prayers and fasting of many, to help end the terrible curse of inequality we are now under. Because everything we do, choose to do, or fail to do, affects all the rest of us to some degree.
Faith and experience have taught me God works through human hands of good will, those who are willing to work together for a better world.

During the more than seventeen years I was able to work in hospitals and Medical Clinics, only felt there was time, energy, to give a little extra, having a family to care for to help support, so did nothing like my heroes of those days, who gave so much, such as Mother Teresa, Gandhi, and many others not widely known.
Such was the son of one of our local Rabbi's, Marshall Ganz a brilliant young man in college. One of many who gave away most promising futures, being in his last year at Harvard, to be able to help make it possible for all races to have the right to vote; to help right our past prejudices and inequalities.
I have known of several, mostly young people, who spent their summers working in civil rights at that time, some didn't return. Many felt called during the time of Martin Luther King, when they realized the importance of helping register first time minority voters, as well as doing sit-downs at lunch counters, where those of color had not been able to eat.

Many were beaten for it, thrown in jail, even killed, some of the young people who helped were white but mostly it was the blacks who lived in the area, who had personally experienced the racism. Knew they did not want to live the rest of their lives under racism. Before allowed to even help in possibly awaken the conscience of others they agree beforehand, to witness Non-Violently, as The Christ Way, being the only way not to become what they wanted to stand against.

Taking place mostly in the Southern part of America, where ancestrally I am from, and still have many family's here and come back usually after many years, to see if much progress has been made among the people here. Most whites at least when in public, do seem to be treating other races now as equal human beings. Still the Civil rights struggle for racial equality has a big need to continue and is expanding to Women's Rights now. One of many rights that need our protection, to help against lots of discrimination.
Not until 1921, long after slavery had ended, before the right to vote became legal for American women. No longer the legal property of males. There are places even here, where they still are considered such with first the Father, than the husband, often only after a paid price or dowery!

Of similar interest to me, when we moved and lived for many years in California, was to hear about a new farm workers movement in Delano, an agricultural area in the San Joaquin Valley, where I went to High School during the same time as Helen Chavez, the pretty wife of Cesar, who with Delores Huerta, another hard-working woman, and with other local labor

26

leaders together Co-founded The United Farm Workers, UFW.

Striking against low wages for long hours in the Valley's desert and deadly hot sun, many other terrible and inhumane working conditions, such as a lack of sanitary facilities, often pesticides exposure, even a lack clean drinking water.
Twice they would end up marching on foot, all 465 miles, to the State Capitol in Sacramento, in a pilgrimage to try to get needed and better working laws.
I wanted to march too, but because of my need to work and final to be able to keep my job or lose my children I didn't get the chance until the second time, not long after Cesar's death.

Both marches started, with less than a 100 willing to walk all the way, yet by the time of finally reaching Sacramento, about a month later, in walking at least 10 miles a day 1000's had heard and joined. In the second March, I finally managed to go, having been very sick and still not feeling well enough, but I asked God to either let me go or let me die, as we passed many farms in the valley, some of the workers would come out when they realized what we we're trying to do.

Walking by on country roads, many would wave, some offered food, others a place to sleep at night. A small truck with our sleeping bags, followed behind us, or sometimes in front. We were met with much love for the most part, once we left Delano, and positive response that only increased as we got closer to Sacramento and more and more people decided to join us. The closer we got to Sacramento, the better I felt. It worked to start my immune system to at least half function again. 10 miles a day, just walking all day.

It had taken the leaders of the farm workers Union many years to just be allowed to legally strike in the fields, not just for themselves but also for those who would come after, who would have to work under driving pressures of being paid by how much and how fast they could move, for many hours, often bending down. So many setbacks, they still continue to struggle for their civil rights, for a better life for all.

Many things around that time helped to end the war in Viet Nam, but surely public protest played a necessary part. Peace vigils we helped to start then, still go on as one war after another continues. I feel more called to witness against the inequality in The Church. Now to the Pope, as being the Head of the largest group of Christians. It is the only way to stop the Patriarchy of inequality.

Inequality affects not only the way those we allow to govern or vote into office. It gives business, especially the power brokers of the International Corporations the seemingly moral right to continue to squeeze ever more profits as possible from the people's wages, as their god become the profits themselves, money becoming more important than people's lives. Half of all people's incomes are already so low many are forced to survive on as little as one meal or less, a very slow but still a starvation diet.

How can any one's daily income be worth 1000's of times more than another's full time labor???

One of us may do little, but how many would it take to insist on an international minimum or maximum? Or at least safety nets of food, shelter for not just the country with the best or most bargaining chips? Who knows what it is possible for people to do! If enough people could see how much immoral belief of inequality and where they start from our belief systems. See how it would be in their best interest to have a fair share for their labor? Could it be by enough believing in Equal Rights, Respect, and an Equal Opportunity according to talent and interest!

Because we think or see primarily in a physical/material world, yet our real Eternal life is constantly on trial in an unseen Spiritual world.

Our bodies of flesh, wear out in less than 100 years for most. Only a Loving, Good God offers the promise of a physical/spirit body in heaven for Eternity!

Who would not want that kind of Hope and Promise? At least to be able to find out how to confirm for yourself, if you could have an Eternal Soul! Few believe anymore partly because of a world of inequality. They will continue to decline as long as there is so much religious male idolatry!

Confirm for yourself if you have kept a clean heart by getting forgiveness for any sin. such as the common social sin of a false male/only image of God or men's idolatry. Possible to confirm if you really live the Universal God given Golden Rule of equally treating others fairly with "Equality". God spoke about our need to end such Discrimination at Vatican II, * in their Pastoral Constitution Art. 29 "to end discrimination for race, sex as not the will of God".

It was 10 years later before I even heard of such a thing. Not until long after the death of Pope John Paul I. Since then, God asked me to go three times, each time to witness to each one of the next three popes. I thought I knew enough Spanish 'um

29

poqueto' to this last Pope but I didn't. He looks and seems so Holy, but a Jesuit, they are the smartest. I want to believe he is, And just has his hands tied behind his back, but I am not sure. And have not asked God and will not. I do know the pressure he is under. I have yet to meet a Jesuit I did not believe wanted to good as well as right! Unlike many others, not so bright or holy. But the sin of Patriarchy they are in to, as are maybe the majority of religious men. The opposite with religious women. Who as consecrated brides of Christ, many yearn only to be one with Jesus in enclosed religious harems. Over 100 I know of Catholic Religious Women, have been also consecrated as Priest legally by at the time Ordained in good standing Bishops, until it became known, a few at the retirement age, were willing. But they are all either or passed away now. The Bishops, in those who were excommunicated from the Roman Catholic Church have formed with thousands of lay people, into the 'Future Church'.

So, like many times historically, God has used nature to bring about a catastrophe. Ask for a Spiritual Rebirth, especially for those who have a hurt soul or feel threatened by others in power. Try to find ways not to support inequality.
Equality in The Church is where God's Morality wants and needs to flow now, could be lost or have to spend many years in purgatory.

The eternal Soul is worth the seeking, the finite physical spirit either dies out or waits to be judged. Heaven can have a chance here as well as there, for Peace and much Joy too.
For Blessings.

31

32

FASTING AT THE VATICAN

This is the fifth day of praying and fasting in St. Peter's Square below the Pope's windows, for an end to inequality and discrimination, where our morality should be flowing from. Psalms 126 tells us to give thanks for all we have. We can give thanks, if for nothing else for the very air we have to breath. 'Those who sow in laughter and song, peace and good deeds, shall reap the richest harvest.' Always in God's better time, not necessarily in ours!

My life has been blessed with much. Most of all with the hope of eternal life. Praise God for that hope! May we live this short life, in Gratitude. Even giving thanks for when it seems like a burden to go through now, believing that what is suffered can be turned towards the means to help us, or others, up another step of a ladder, even possible to enter heaven in this life, as well as the next.

'Nothing need be wasted'; if the worse can be turned to good, then it is a good reason to seek God's Hand, especially in times of stress. Also turned to 1 Peter in the New Testament, Chapter 5. Once at a mountain retreat, a Monk Priest had confirmed my habit of turning to pages within scriptures to try to fit a current need. Creating a picture in words of what I would recognize I needed to know at that time. Coincidence? Well, it must then confirm with the Golden Rule for it is easy to take Scriptures out of context, that might only apply to their times or ways, or be reflecting their own image culturally!

This time I turned to where St. Peter spoke to the elders: "Feed the flock willingly, not feeling forced or just for money but with a ready mind. Not to be as Lord's over what is God's but to be the better example".
Then to the younger ones, he says: "Be the better example of which you are. All are to be subject to one another, wearing the clothing of humility, for God rejects and allows the proud to stumble but gives grace to the humble."

Could I be here fasting and praying in this sackcloth and not feel humbled?
Strangely enough there is also a sense of being close to heaven, not in a physical present-day situation but in a spiritual sense that is difficult to describe, just sometimes a little sight, or feeling of the hope yet to be, so I must wait for God's Holy Spirit to give me more direction.

The Pope had surprised me by actually stopping in front of me next to the last time I could be in St. Peters. Because of my shyness and the unexpectedness of his actually stopping, after not stopping for the past two and a-half months of Wednesday audiences of many thousands in St. Peters Square. I seemed tongue tied and could not use my voice and only barely managed to hand him my poem on "Equality". I had only seen him actually stop a couple of times before, and then seemingly just to be photographed with babies held out to him.
After this experience I was determined I would speak, if God would somehow allow him to stop again! Would you

believe the next week, the very last week I could possibly be there, He did stop again and right in front of me again!
But this time a gorgeously dressed beautiful young woman dripping with fine jewels, was noisily trying to squeeze in between us.

He seemed, not only distracted but also annoyed, and when I did find the courage to speak when He looked at me in the eyes. I spoke and after a moment He just motioned for one of his aides to hand me a prayer card of Jesus as a young boy, about 3 years old, but naked!

Ah, a third leg needed, had been his planned response!

Good Grief, how else can I get through to him now?

A quote from Patrice Tuohy's "Divine Wisdom"

"At times Biblical Poetry sets theological distinctions aside. In some places, in Hebrew Scripture, for example, Divine wisdom is feminine, spoken of in a way indistinguishable From God."

Those who have studied theology know that the word "Father" when used for God includes the "Mother", but not so many others, as it seems to have been well kept from those who have not had a chance to understand or had thought of it as important to check for themselves.

Therein lies much misinformation, false assumptions!

God being male only, in many people's Image of God creates the sin of Idolatry the worship of a false Image of God. The number one sin of the Ten Commandments, forbidden to

Jews, Christians, as well as Muslims. Yet have you in our many patriarchal cultures ever heard anything about it preached?

Think I was sent all the way to The Holy Land to learn about this Truth. In my heart I had known it. Logic said it had to be true, but I had little for sure concrete scientific evidence for it. What is the original meaning of Father without having a Mother?

The best Good News I learned while in The Holy Land and still want to share about the One Lord God, Our Christian Lord, as Jesus Christ being part of The Only God worthy of worshiping, is also called our "Heavenly Parent", the literal definition of what Jesus called "God, ABBA = Heavenly Parent", Dad-AB&BA-Mom. Or ABBA."

From the official Aramaic in Biblical days and spoken by most living in the Holy Land. As Hebrew was considered more sacred and reserved for the Temple and Synagogues. And taught to Hebrew males only.

God as our Mother as well as Father, as well as Christ, A Child of God. Just as we too were created in the earliest Biblical Scriptures of the first and third Creation stories in Gen. 1:37 and Gen. 5:1 that tell us "both male and female created in the Image of God".

This is the Theology of what we call the Trinity in our Patriarchal languages called Father, Son and Holy Spirit. As Holy Spirit in Hebrew being primarily a feminine word The Mother of God.

God as well as humans, are Biblically characterized in terms of Father, Mother, Child or Son, and duplicated in human beings. As each physically we each have all the hormones, organs only in different amounts at different times and sometimes in different places or slightly different depending on our sexual natures for the purpose of reproduction, at least for humans. Such as the male sexual organ is normally outside the body, the female counterpart or vagina is within, ending in the Womb, the womb being the only organ not duplicated in the male human body.

Well enough about the physiology of our natures, was wanting to show the similarity between God and Creation of humans as all are personally Children of God, as far as I know. My information learned over many years in study and working in Medicine, both Orthodox and Naturalistic.

March 11, 2011

Vatican City,
Holy Father Pope Benedict XVI,

It is the first day of spring, one of the most promising days of the year. A day to take a lesson from nature, that we will now have equal amounts of both day and night.

A time for us humans to be as equals, especially in our Church, where Christ morality should be flowing.
Out of this winter of inequality that has caused so much disparity, where half of the world's population is in process of starvation!

Our Church sets the example with the Universal beliefs of The Golden Rule, especially for the female half of God's Image.

With the guidance and direction of The Holy Spirit I must give you this message, at St. Peter's Square, in April 2011, when I will be there in Rome, pleading for your help, as you are the only one who can set a moral example at this time for the less than 2% of those, who now control over 90% of our worlds wealth and see nothing wrong with this lack of inequality. Because the Church still allows, and practices it, yet you know it is not from God, for God is a God of equity.

I have read several of your books and a message on Equality from the Day of peace for 2004. It is now time we all become more Christ like, before more people are allowed to starve.

Your friend in Christ, Betty C Dudney

GOD AS THE BREATH OF LIFE

Boundless and without end, God can be known as
Infinite, Freeing

LOVE, PEACE, and JOY.

A HOLY LOVE, EQUITY, A GOD who is
"Not a god of partiality".

Only God worthy of worship cannot have a negative
Spirit, nor is the cause of evil.

Some causes are the act of putting one's self above
an equal concern for others.

God is One, infinite, yet can Live in each heart.

Trying to break free from my own cultural
conditioned kind of thinking, to be able to express
more of God's way of "Equality" thinking.

Knowing words can be so easily misunderstood.
Partly by where our hearts or motives are, but also
from where our morality comes from, morals that have
been accepted since Biblical times when slavery,
sexism was the patriarchal way of believing, their own
Truth, and Reality.

Even for those at the very top of the pyramid
of control, there is still a lack of equality, up to gross

inequality, that is being enforced by their laws, from their patriarchal traditional ways.

Our cultural truths, realities are learned from conditionings, of hearing, seeing, the kinds of knowing that come into the senses, sometimes repeated over and over until it sinks in, on a subconsciously as well as conscious level, then they become a truth, a reality of our experience.

Partly why there are so many different versions of beliefs of the Higher Self, we were as humans created in the Image of.

Once I had realized this, God's given word of "Equality" became a much more convincing concept of our world, for us to be able to live in peace, as well as a much needed concept of love and security in regards to each other.

There are no Islands that are isolated any more, No safe underground cities to take refuge, hide it. And never were walls high enough where we could not be affected by what others who were strong enough could do!

This past week's general audience in St. Peter's Square with Pope Benedict XVI was the best so far as I did manage to get this prayer to one of his aides as He drove by, high up in the Pope Mobile.

DIVINE WISOM AS FEMININE TOO

FOR EQUAL HUMAN RIGHTS
ESPECIALLY WITHIN THE CHURCH
FROM WHERE GOD'S MORALITY FLOWS
LORD HEAR OUR PRAYER

FOR EQUAL HUMAN RESPECT
THE BALANCING OF UN-BALANCE-NESS
FROM DISCRIMINATION AND PREJUDICE
OH LORD HEAR OUR PRAYER

FOR EQUAL HUMAN CONCERN
TO END THE PRESENT INEQUALITY
A WAY TO BRING BACK MANY TO GOD
LORD HEAR OUR PRAYER

FOR MUTUAL OPPORTUNITY
THE HOLY SPIRIT SPOKE IN VATICAN II
SPEAKS STILL TO ALL GOOD HEARTS

This is the same poem I gave to John Paul II in 1985, the first time of witnessed for three months here in Rome, before going on to Israel for what I through God was sending me to do there, a Peace Scroll.

42

ON TO THE HOLY LAND

Needed to find just the best affordable place to stay, but not until after my first month as a pilgrim in this my European ancestral roots as a Huguenot Christian, first within the 14th Century French Convent, on the Via Del Rosa, as The Way of the Cross, within the Arab section of the Old City of Jerusalem.

That first night the taxi from the plane in Tel Aviv, let me off at the Donkey Gate, opening into a too narrow street for cars, of the Old City. The convent being only a short walk down the little street, actually between the Second and Third Stations of the Cross. The First station I expected to be only a few steps from where I was let off. With just my suitcase and a backpack yet my seeing only a few poorly dressed young thin men there standing around, who then started to gather around me as soon as the taxi left, and I began to fear.

Would you believe they only came up to see if they could be of help! Once I gave them the address they insisted on carrying everything for me. I would learn these young men were the best a stranger to their land could want to welcome me to the Holy Land.

Typical of many young and older women here too! While most of them have little of life's material things, all I met had such a precious willingness to be helpful.

Pretty much come to think of it, like most of the youth I've known, where-ever I have been!

They joyfully carried all my weight and then waited at the

door with me, until someone finally answered to let me in. It was late, around 10 pm by then. They even refused to take any money for their help!

May God bless them wherever they are? Surely not many of them could feel very safe with our world as it is, seems even more so now but even then it must have been daily scary for these young Arab men living there.

The Old City, at least at that time in 1986, was divided into three sections for the three religious' offshoots, all being of Abraham's descendants, Jewish, and Muslims having about an equal number, with a smaller Christian section partly separating the two. Jerusalem is very much a Holy City for all three of these Religions.

Outside the large Old City walls of Jerusalem, on two sides, the much larger city itself extends into a large Muslim and Jewish residential areas, with just a few Christian groups found beyond the giant tall thick walls of the Old City.

Bethlehem, the little city of Jesus birth is only two miles away and almost completely Arab, but now have heard it has been walled off from Jerusalem, surrounded with more thick walls of Jewish settlements in between.

The closed Golden Gate is on the east side of the walled Old City, I have heard it will not be opened, the Jews believe until the Messiah returns. It is not that far from the open Donkey Gate, both facing the Mount of Olives.

Steep cliffs and sparsely settled valleys can be seen Western side. While I lived there they had begun to excavate Solomon's steps just outside those walls that would have led directly into the Temple, that had existed during the time of King David and his son King Solomon.

Evidence there is room for the Temple to be rebuilt at its former location in this end of mostly vacant Temple Mount and still contain for Muslims, the Golden Dome Mosque that had been built on the rock behind the Wailing Wall and another near the outside wall.

It is a standoff of selfishness, for anyone to be thinking only their beliefs are important enough or only they have a right to worship or live there. Yet it has been part of the purpose mainly of the political right in Israel, to drive their brothers or ancestral cousins the Arabs off this land.

Not likely this could happen without an all-out war, as this is The Mount where Muslims believe Mohammad ascended into Heaven, a very Holy site for them too!

It is going to take at the least a sense of "Equality" on both sides, for either side to come out winners, until then we all will remain in great danger. If we have a nuclear war now or in the near future, those left would most likely be killed by radiation fall out after and would have to live for an unknown length of time with little modern amenities left.

In other word's most of us would be forced back to a very primitive lifestyle, more a desert or mean like jungle. Revelation Prophecy speaks of Christ not returning until the allotted time for evil has ended. * 6 both Chapters 12,13 of Revelations.

45

These are prophetic end time years, since the time of Christ which may be as much as another five to six hundred years or more from our present time, depending on where the beginning of the time is calculated from, from around the Birth of Jesus or the beginning of the early Church, or even from the first officially recognized Church in Rome.

What is important to realize is we have no way of knowing for sure and have to consider the Biblical "soon" *7 can easily be in God's Time a thousand years, as like a day or two.

*7 II Thess. 2:2-4

Christians using the excuse that they can just wait for Jesus to return and don't need to do their share to make this a better place for all to be, are misjudging what Jesus said about how we each would be judged to enter Heaven; by what we did to or failed to do for the least. *8 Matt. 25:40-45

After World War II the League of Western Nations gave the land of Palestine to be a Jewish State so they might be able to have a homeland because of all they had suffered in Germany during the war.

The League of Nations intentions were those living there would be compensated for any land needed. Not considering that few Arabs have been willing to sell their birthrights to the land they too cherish, as their own ancestral homeland, nor did they realize the large number of Palestinians who were already living there at the time. Not only in Bethlehem but in many areas for centuries around and in the country around the Sea of Galilee.

Either, to justify the land taken, and/or to continue reaping wartime contract profits, the Corporate owned media helped spread propaganda the Holy Land was only sparsely populated, to downplay how many Arabs were actually living there.

Israel has now taken much of the land by force and many of the Arab ancestral homes have been bulldozed, with little compensation given, especially if they tried to protest often there was none given according to the stories I heard! Picture yourself in their shoes, what would you have done, or would do?

Have you seen the young people who faced the tanks and the bulldozers with only rocks in their hands? Terrorist? There is no easy way now, to a Peace settlement between these ancestral brothers or cousins, partly because of the violent actions that happened on both sides.

Violence only begets more revengeful violence. It can be stopped only by controlled non-violence! Is there something you can do? God's Holy Spirit can tell you in your heart what that is, but only if you are really willing to be open to a solution, to listen, and then to answer that call.

The Torah, Bible, and Koran and Christian Scriptures all say God's people are not to oppress those who have chosen to live on the land.

A Palestinian State for the Arabs would maybe help, as well as sufficient compensation for homes that were bulldozed, but the wounds are deep. I have found it increasingly appalling that the Palestinians have been treated more like the Jews were treated under German rule.

Crowded into similar concentration like camps they too had endured, but now are called refuge's camps some near the Dead

Sea area and for miles on the West Bank.

Appalled that my country, the United States, continues to support this injustice and has even financially made it possible, by the giving of military aid just to Israel. So many not knowing this, wonder why there are Arab terrorist?
Or why 9/11 happened?

We continue to hear on the news, only what the media wants us to hear. Yet wouldn't you try to fight too, or do what you could, if someone came to your area with the force to bulldoze you and your Neighbors homes?

In the time of my being there the Holy Land was in an uneasy peace, of armed Israeli Soldiers patrolling the streets with Rifles and side guns.

In a small courtyard of the old city, part of the then Christian/Armenian section, I did find my own little studio apartment I could afford, just across an alley from the Armenian Monastery, where I would also find the library.

One day after much questioning, the librarian brought out for me to see, a very old Dictionary containing the oldest record of Aramaic words. In the ancient language the people and Jesus spoke, in those Biblical days.

The Librarian was pleased at my delight to see for the first time for myself, the word Jesus used for God, "ABBA" actually meant "Heavenly Parent" and includes the familiar definition of Mom as well as Dad. It also is one of the few words of the original Aramaic language left in the English Bibles, the language Jesus normally spoke, that has been translated into Patriarchal languages, including English and most others.

The other Aramaic words I read were those Jesus used to raise the little girl Tabatha, from the dead. It would be interesting to know what those original words mean too? But at the time it was enough for me to find out Jesus was not a sexist!

The translators must have realized, the consequences a patriarchal language would have on the culture but left only those original words for ab evidence of their true meaning.

Jesus was not using a false Image of God and did not call God the English translated word of "Father" where it has been translated. So why are we being taught to?

We need to be using a non-sexist language. It would help us to be able to come out of our present day "Idolatry" and the inequality our world is still caught up in and is perpetuating!

Have only been able to find in the best editions of English Webster Dictionaries, the word "Father" when applied to God is not defined just as a male god, but like the word men, includes the concept of women, or includes the mother as well as the father. "Heavenly Parent" would be another correct definition.

Even though God is spoken of as One, would have both male and female qualities, as the Christian Trinity expresses sexual equality if you know the Word for Holy Spirit of God was originally a feminine word, coming from the same Hebrew root word as wind or "Yah Ruah", The Breath of God. From "EL".

The trinity in Christianity usually called Father, Son, and Holy Spirit, can also be expressed as Father, Mother, and Child.

In most minds by using only the male pronouns such as "He" or "Father", in effect does creates a false, male only, Image of God, within the mind from reading, speaking, or hearing, and can then easily be used to justify sexism and inequality. Maybe one reason Jewish Religious only write of God as G-D?

Knowing only for sure I was to go to the Holy Land, I had assumed God wanted me to do a Peace Scroll, because there was so much tension and sporadic violence there in 1985 and they seemed still so close to an even more terrible war. It was much later before realizing it was the meaning of the word "ABBA" that I needed to find the evidence of the word that Jesus used for God. For it is the original word that counts, and the true definition we need to be using too.

The most original documents we have now as Christian Scriptures are hand-written copies, and only those decided upon by the Roman Catholic Church, primarily in the third and fourth centuries. The writings before that time, those that became an actual part of the New Testament where not kept with the exception of a few from the letters of Paul. Why?

There is only speculation. Ranging from their fragility to knowing only males were allowed to do the writing or editing under the official control of The Emperor in His Roman Empire in those most patriarchal times.

The versions of Creation and most Hebrew Scriptures were written, most likely long after the time, coming from the oral traditions of their twelve Hebrew tribes, passing the tales down at campfires, again by males only, unknown years before being written down, many of the moral stories or parables.

There are still nomadic desert tribes called Bedouins, in the Holy Land, they come into the cities for trading, often with their camels and own desert forms of oral traditions. I would spend precious time talking to one proprietor of a little store near the first station.

Within a week of arriving in Jerusalem, I met a woman after Church Services in the Olive Garden Tomb, dug out of the side of the mountain, not far from outside the Damascus Gate of the Old City, where you can still see the Skull of Golgotha, and only a couple blocks away from this skull, across from what was known then as the Arab bus station.

The Garden Tomb is a large garden with the crystal cave, believed to be where Jesus lay. A room with four sides, floor and ceiling, all the walls dug out of pure solid white crystal rock in the side of this mountain.

A raised space dug out of the crystal floor for the length of the originally planned master's body, had later, at the end of the wall, been hastily dug out, about a foot longer and wider, for a different body size than the rich owner of this rare crystal burial site.

Making it even more believable and astonishing to me, that this could have been the actual burial site of Jesus, was noticing, in this pure white all crystal room, just a cup sized reddish brown looking scorch on the place where the chest or heart might have laid.

Would it be possible this seemly slight burnt like mark in the crystal floor, might have been where the heart had been zapped by a lightening like bolt, to bring back Jesus heart to life?

There was also a dug out a long gully in the front of this cave room where a huge round stone had once been rolled across the entrance. The Christian sign of the "Fish" that is known as an ancient symbol of the then persecuted secret Christian site, deep within the huge Olive Garden carved above the entrance and believed to have been used later as a meeting place for Christians during the first several hundred years of Christian persecution.

Here within the safety of this wealthy man's large Olive Garden, where still there are parts left of a large olive press and would have then provided much wealth from the sale of olive oil to this area as it was used not only for cooking, but also for the only evening light with oil lamps.

Once it is seen, experienced, it leaves little doubt this beautiful garden could have been the one owned by the secret rich disciple Joseph of Arimathea, who already had a tomb already close to the Cross, that he used to bury Jesus in and like the described place of his resurrection, also spoken of in scriptures, just a short distance from the outside of the Old City and the Damascus Gate where you can see the Skull of Golgotha where they crucified the two others with Jesus.

Now the orchard is owned by the Church of England. Almost daily open to the public. I started talking to a lady after the service as we had set next to each other, she told me about a vacancy with an Archeological dig at the near-by Rockefeller Institute where She worked and knew of a need for a part time worker, exactly what I needed to find. Praise God, how needs can be met when we are willing to walk within God's Hand, while trying to do God's Will, but again in God's time, not always in ours.

Working at the Archeological dig I met another woman who was visiting from New Zealand, and found she was willing to help me in the gathering of the signatures for a Peace Scroll, after we both finished our morning job at the dig, which was only about a mile out of town.

This is the same Valley, outside of Jerusalem where the young David is said to have killed the Giant threatening his people, with only a rock and his slingshot, who later became one of the few "good" Kings they would have.

We were working on a Roman Villa that many centuries later had been built in that windy valley. She did help me with the Peace Scroll for many months until her visa ran out, but just about the time we felt there were enough signatures!

Over 5000 from such a variety of people, locals of all beliefs, as well as tourist, who would agree: "For Peace we will treat others with Equal Respect and Concern", Signing their name and the town or country they were from.

To make the Scrolls, I had used two long rolling pins, toping them on the ends with four beautifully decorated Olive-wood candlesticks I had found in the many market stands that line the little inner streets of the Old City. Using a roll of butcher's paper around the rolls to gather the signatures. We gathered them

53

beside the gates of the Old City, depending on where we felt it was safest to go on that day.

Both of us were very grateful when we felt we had gathered so many and felt it was enough, partly because of the occasional scary and even narrow avoidance of serious incidences, at least two miraculous happenings. One a bomb at the Damascus Gate that killed 17 people. I would have been there and was going by myself that day, except I felt led to go to the lower less traveled gate for some needed vegetables first, because they were cheaper there, and would have probably been sold out if had waited to go later.

Hearing the explosion so close from there, I was too shaken up to go, as I should have done, having had nurse's training, but felt it had been meant for me and instead cowered all the way home through the narrow alleyways.

Yet another time, again by myself, a group of about 8-9 PLO male "Terrorist" surrounded me at the Damascus Gate, with their knives drawn.
The Holy Spirit must have been the one to speaking to them, for it did not seem like my voice at all and because they did calm down ending up only cutting the parchment paper part of the Scroll, with great big X's.

After all that trouble of getting and then giving the Scrolls to who they needed to go to, there was not even a single response, from any of them!
And the situation in that part of the world still remains today a powder keg.

It was not just Our efforts for Peace, at least once a month, there would be Peace Vigils, sometimes hundreds would gather,

Arabs, Jews, and Christians would come together peacefully in the city.

Once I remember walking with them to the Prime Ministers house, where we had a twilight vigil with candles, again no response.

An international action helped to create the lack of peace there and it will take the Inter-national community I believe to solve it. Preventing a nuclear holocaust is in everybody's interest.

Equal Human Rights is the key, the equal value of each person's rights to life, liberty, and the freedom to be, as long as they are not trampling on the rights of others.

In my personal relationship with God, after gaining the knowledge from the Monastery Library of God not originally being a male only god in the definition of the words, has made a great difference in my feelings and a more personal loving relationship with Jesus as well as God. Also, in realizing the importance of this one Word of "Equality", I have come to believe this was the main purpose for the seven Precious months, of my being able to live in The Holy Land.

Even though I had a very loving and good human Dad, as well as a good Mom, and can't imagine what my relationship with God would be like if I hadn't. Or what I would be feeling, if I had to believe God was male only.

Would assume it could go either way, depending on what kind of parents one may have had, it could make it very difficult to want to know, or even be able to feel, a love for God as your Heavenly Parent, after having had an unloving parent.

Most importantly for males it seems to have tended to create a false sense of superiority about being a male, as well as give females a sense of inferiority, about their own self and each other!

Realizing God is Our Heavenly Parent, including the traits of both our Mother, as well as Father, can't help but make a lot of difference in how we treat each other too.

During the time spent there I also learned those in power, the major Political and/or Religious Party, believe they have or had a secret "Messiah", with them. A Jewish neighbor, in trying to convince me to join the Jewish community or at least to turn away from Christianity, told me this, very convincingly.

He said their "Messiah" had performed supernatural cures for their top religious leaders and described doing several things of what I thought could have been more like Magician's tricks especially since he has encouraged them for many years now, to continue their violence and inequality against the Arabs.

I would say if he really is influencing their Religious and political Leaders as a "Messiah", he is much more likely to be what Christians think of, as an antichrist, or evil one who would or could have even supernatural powers.

It was very discouraging after so much effort in doing the Peace Scroll, to realize it probably wasn't going to affect their belief in this "Messiah" and that they were going to continue to drive out their Arab ancestral brothers or cousins from the land, especially if we continue our support of it.

Land, they both have lived on since Abraham, most of the time in Peace. It seems we will remain close to a nuclear

Holocaust.

Not only can we not know the day or hour, and not even the actual year or month, that will end the rule of evil on our planet, but we can pretty much know it is not likely to be in our normal thinking of the Biblical word "soon".

Yet we do have the power to change the worse of prophecy and is why it is given, for those willing to do what they can, but only for those willing to do God's Will rather than just their own.

A nuclear war near or at this time in our history, would make for a hellish miserable world, maybe for hundreds of years for those and their children who might survive it.

That is why the importance in our time of "Equality" among nations and peoples, to be able to avoid otherwise likely more nuclear mishaps, or wars, or even crazy people in control of buttons, not to mention leaks!

Yet I was being assured by one of their "Black Hatter's", who had never read Christian Scriptures or that prophecy, that they have The Messiah or "Christ".

Many do not know or believe Jesus was from God, or was The Christ, so they are not likely to believe in our Christian Prophecy.

The only thing I could think of to counter with, was according to our Christian Scriptures, when Christ returned, it would be for everyone to know, and The Messiah would be seen by all. *9 Matt. 24:3

The Messiah or Christ would not be hidden or come in secret, or would not come for just one race, but would come equally for all those who would allow a Godly Love into their hearts. As I have reason to believe God Is "not a god of partiality", God's Love is for all, found in both the Jewish, Muslim as well as Christian Scriptures. Doubt I said or knew then to specifically say much of that to him.

We tend to stumble even on easy paths to righteousness and satisfaction from feelings of doing a good job and do always benefit from God's Help. Eventually realizing we were not as smart as we thought or would like to be.

Whether we continue stumbling or sinking in mud is up to us. Sometimes a Guardian Angel will try to push you forward. We really do live best, in better or less of times, by believing in having God's Help, to keep from being overrun by the world's ways. Let God be your refuge, place of shelter.

HUMANS MAKE MISTAKES, AND MISJUDGE,
THANK GOODNESS GOD DOES NOT.

59

"English: Pray for an end to inequality, especially within The Church from where morality from God should flow first! Read in all languages. www.equality4peace.org

Italian: Pregare per la fine di diseguaglianza, in particolare all'internodella Chiesa, da dove la morale da Dio dovrebbe fluire primo!Letto in tutte le lingue www.equality4peace.org

German: Beten Sie für ein Ende Ungleichheit, vor allem innerhalb derKirche, von wo aus die Moral von Gott fließen sollen zuerst! Lesen Sie in allen Sprachen. www.equality4peace.

French: Priez pour la fin de l'inégalité, en particulier au sein de l'église d'où la morale de Dieu devrait premier flux! Lire dans toutes les langues. www.equality4peace.org

Japanese: 不平等に終止符のための祈りは、
教会、特に内から神からの道徳は、
最初に流れる必要がありますここで！
www.equality4peace.orgですべての言語で読

　　Used these and similar cards, to give out to people who would stop to talk to me, while fasting and praying at the fountain in St. Peter's Square, in Rome witnessing. Not many would stop, but a few, more at the Wednesday audiences and there I would try to pass out as many as possible.

Twice the Vatican police forced me leave, just for handing them out. Still, I would come back the next day. Often would then stay nearby, sometimes driving in front or back and even occasionally very close, but most of the time they would leave me alone. The antichrist I find tends to work in all religions, for that is where most unconverted souls are, who are not already or yet partly at least under his control.

Within the Vatican, besides The Pope, there are two other blocks of little-known power, the Vatican police, separate from The Swiss Guards, as are The Pope's personal bodyguards. It is the Police who carry the firearms, and under the control of the elected President of The Vatican State, whose elected job is the running of what is known as Vatican City.

Roma, Italia
May 23, 2011

Dear Holy Father Pope Benedict XVI,

It always seems incredulous to go from a miserable day to a Blessed Day, but that is what has happened to me on this special day!
Even though it is beginning to rain again, had a chance to talk to a woman, who had seemed to understand what I was doing here with my sackcloth, with the cross on it that has the

equal = sign as the cross bars, although we both had made a few attempts to communicate before, more than recognizing each other as praying friends.

I have been seeing her at the fountain where I usually go for several hours to say my rosaries, while looking up at your Windows far above and after first coming out of St. Peters, usually to go to mass.

Even with her little bit of English and my poquito, or um poi Italian, we have finally managed to understand each other enough to know that about 3 years ago, she had a vision from God about The Church needing to accept women as equals, and while I had been told by God's Holy Spirit the one word of "Equality" many years ago, in my second encounter with God.

My first encounter, over 25 years before that, was when I was shown The Hand of God, I believe at so young an age, to keep me from ever thinking it was from any of my own merit.

Kind of like when Eli was called by God, as a child. We know God calls many in their early years, in some way.

So, Praise God, I see this meeting with this other Witness as not only a confirmation for an end to inequality within the Church from where God wishes God's morality to flow from first.

Now have something more to deal with, to understand what this means! You may already know this, as she says she is in touch with your private Secretary, a Monsignor by a similar sounding last name as one I know in America, who I even went to see before coming here, for his Blessing.

I know she is telling the truth about the name, because I had received a response with his name on it, as having received a letter about a year ago, that I had written to you from America. As I did request a signature at a much greater expense but with a little more assurance it actually has been received in your office.

This Monsignor in America that I do know, I had also seen and had a miracle encounter with when I first came to Rome to witness about inequality in 1985, and to see the then Pope John Paul II, who did the opposite of what I had tried to tell him God was sending me to Rome for, of our great need to end inequality within The Church. He made it instead that much harder.

A few years later I was shown, after asking God why, a vision of him with his hands tied behind his back and a knife in midair!

The miracle with the Monsignor Priest, also in Rome happened in 1985, because I had been visiting Rome's different Church's outside the Vatican, not only to go to mass and to visit but also to look for evidence of Saints who had been preserved after death, but had found only one, who really looked still fully preserved.

He looked so well preserved, even up very close as I could sit beside the all glass, coffin for long periods of time and did, in trying to decide if maybe this he was for real or if it could be a wax reproduction?

This was the former Cardinal St. Giuseppe Maria Tomase of about 500 years ago, the son of a Prince from Sicily, who had given up his rich worldly life to then become a servant within the Church.

When I heard he was going to be canonized at St. Peter's, I felt I had to go and while there asked for a sign, for one of the numerous miracles that happen to some who pray or witness the canonization of a Saint.

The miracle I asked for seemed it could be fairly simple for a new Saint, his such a Spiritual name as it was just to see my Priest Friend while he was still in Rome since I would have to leave in a week or so, to go on to the Holy Land.

Knowing he was in Rome on a Sabbatical, but had no idea where? Had thought I had seen him once walking out of St. Peter's with another Priest; but my shyness had prevented me from running after, to be able possibly to catch up with him.

Now thinking surely we could just meet on the way out of this special St. Peters Mass! Yet would I have believed it had been a miracle if that was the way it happened?

When it did not happen then I began thinking it really must have been a wax representation, and feeling tired and let down, so went home to take a nap, had to go home way out on the edge of Rome as the most reasonable apartment I had been able to find for the only three months I would be able to live in Rome.

After only about 15 min. of lying down, I suddenly felt wide-awake with a new strong feeling to get up and go to see the beach! This would take at least an hour trip by train even after I got back to the main train station in Rome!

I had seen most of the city of Rome but had not seen the Mediterranean Sea fairly close by, so it did seem like a good idea.

Yet not really having enough extra money to do this, still the urging was strong I took off, first going back into town, where I had just come from, then to find ad get on a train to the beach, and after arriving there, could only see to walk across the sands straight to the water's edge, where others were walking a fairly short distance away, turned to the right to start walking in the sand. Soon coming to a little tiny bridge that crossed a small stream running into the sea. As I got to the top arch of it, here was this Priest I had been looking for, walking right in front of me with another Priest. Only coming from the opposite direction!

We both were a little stunned as I tried to explain in the moment or two we stood there, holding up a steady stream of people behind both of us who were also wanting to walk over this little bridge, but just a moment for both of us to say a very surprised hello, good to see you, then the three of us continued down the bridge on our own separate ways.

I could only take the first path back to the train, to go back to Rome, still partly in a daze, for I had Really seen, experienced fully my Miracle.

Yet when I got back on the train, here they were again, already sitting, having gotten on the stop before in the other direction where I had gotten off from.

So, this time after he explained to his friend, he came over and sat down beside me. As I had sat down near them on the same car, to hopefully be able to explain a little more in detail how my seeing him had come about.

I don't know if he told or explained to the other Priest, or would he even be able to believe it? But the two of us for sure knew and knew we believed!

Since coming back here have not been able to put all the pieces together yet, how this is to work or what exactly God has in mind, but it is sure more than coincidence for her to be here, and I'm elated for it is another sign that God is leading the way. If she is another witness as she says she too feels called to witness for "Equality" within The Church from her vision.

She says you are in agreement, and in her conversations with your secretary arranged for her a place to stay, to be able to pray here at the Vatican and has been for several hours each day at this same fountain here under your office windows. Am I wrong to be thinking God had me come here again just to be able to witness with her? Feel there is so much need to explain and best to you!

Raised as a Protestant, I learned much about Scriptures and so much more when God led me to the Catholic Church, eventually to being confirmed as a convert in 1975. Have learned to love this Church so could not stand the bad that I also see in it, even tried to leave once by turning away and walking back towards where I then lived one Sunday morning while walking to mass, only a few blocks away. Once more I would experience God's Hand, this time only to feel it in mine, and looking down at my own hand, could not see it, only feel it in mine, as it spun me back in my tracks and back towards the Church.

There is no doubt in my mind God wants me to be in this Church to help it be the best it can be. I now can better understand God's Wisdom of why!

The only other major contact I have had with God came at my Spiritual "Rebirth" at about 29 years old; Jesus spoke of our need for Spiritual "Rebirths".

Intellectually I had had doubts since college, the reality of God's intelligence, existence, or even concern with our puny lives. Plus, all the bad things that seem to happen even to good people. Forgetting that we live in world where the sun shines on the bad as well as the good, and the rain does the same. Depending so much on where we happen to be at the time and spiritually places are not the same as physical places.

Or maybe a better way to say it one must learn to have the trust of a child to eventually be able to "See" a better way, reason, or purpose for what happens to us as individuals.

Yet in remembering seeing God's Hand, when I was young, felt I had to know for sure, one way or another, so I asked for a "fleece". Fasted and prayed when I could for two weeks.

At the end, on a Sunday, I sat down in an easy chair, my children with their father, visiting their grandparents. I said to myself "Well I cannot fast or pray anymore, I guess there is no God, or surely I would have had a sign by now".

Immediately though the walls of the room came God's Spirit, not only filling up the room but also fully washing over me and I heard clearly the one distinct word of "EQUALITY".

Since then, have studied fully the meaning of this word of "Equality" and it's many analogies, such as "God is not a god of partiality" and many similar Scriptural Words such as God's Equity, Equal Justice, as well as Equal Rights, including Equal Opportunity! An Equal Concern for each other we need to live the best possible life. Have also tried my best to live it, as well as avoid the evil of any inequality.

"Praise God", each one of us are uniquely made, yet each special, and equally loved by God!

With males only in control most of our religions are so unbalanced, it seems hard for many, to even see the damage it is doing to our world.

It gives a rationalization for the secular world, to continue, not only to discriminate against the female half, but more than over half of All people being affected economically by the gross inequality from the corporate greed of inequality.

Our world economy now being 90% owned by less than 5%, believed by many to be closer to only 2%.

As well as controlling the world's resources that God created to be used for all. At the least, not to have half our world on a starvation diet mostly because of this belief and practice of inequality.

It cannot possibly be God's Will for our Church to continue to practice inequality, it has to be stopped, as it makes it so hard for others to believe or practice the Good News that is preached, but still not being practiced.

A friend in Christ,

Betty C. Dudney

69

HALF-WAY THROUGH

The last Day of April, am half-way through this
Prayer and Fasting, just couldn't put on sackcloth, or
fast today and very little Prayer. Fighting off a cold, it
has been raining again, most of the day.

Thought earlier about trying to go to the Vatican,
and even ventured out between rains this morning
to see how strong I felt about walking, but ended up
spending most of the day in bed, with just a little on the
computer.
Trying to rewrite a not so good poem did many
years ago, called "Idolatry" of which there seems to be
much going on here, with the Image of the late Pope
John Paul II, much bigger than life, plastered all over
this town.

Even between the numerous columns that line St.
Peter's Square! As well as in many of the Church's
throughout the City of Rome.
Huge outdoor movie screens continuously show his
Image, telling of his many trips worldwide and
showing him being adored by thousands upon many
thousands wherever he went.
I want to say for what? For putting women back in their
"place"? Putting the reputation of The Church, above the safety
and welfare of children?

Keeping half of our world in a state of hunger?

I wish I were not feeling this way and I know I may be misjudging him. Think part of it is my over-all mood of not feeling good right now. Although if it were not for God's insistence, would not have stayed within this Church, and then would not feel so personally concerned about what is happening here.

Many progressive Catholics have left after it became obvious Vatican II was not going to become more than window dressing.

For those "right or wrong, my church" members and the more heavily indoctrinated cradle Catholics, many who were taught to believe "The Church" can do no wrong, I am well aware that making any criticism of a Pope is at the least, considered very disrespectful. Yet I can't help thinking about our first Pope after Vatican II, John Paul I and his unexpected and untimely death.

Pope John Paul II took his name, and promised to hundreds of Sisters, and Religious, who came to appeal once again to their Pope in 1979, to end discrimination as the other Pope John Paul I had said should be done. Then only a few years later this Pope does just the opposite?

Is the antichrist so strongly entrenched here in the Vatican? St. Paul spoke of the antichrist being even in the Church in Biblical times. So why wouldn't it still be here?

Where else would demons work harder, to try to be the most effective than in worldwide religious organizations?
Best not judge the motives of others, just judge my own way, in our own thinking we can confirm what is good or not, by the universal Golden Rule alone.

Yet some amount of judging the fruits of others is necessary where we are involved or affected. A touchy balance that carries sometimes a heavy cost for misjudging if one is culpable or not, in judging. How much was known and when, is really not the point of asking, it is to make conscious our need to deal with so many dictatorial hierarchies, and top-heavy pyramid systems whether they are in religious, political, or economic areas that exert so much control over our lives, giving so many places for the antichrist to become embedded, and making it easier for all to be exploited.

It is so hard to reach those at the top who make the crucial decisions as they get surrounded by others who tend to work hard to keep any bad or what they see as negative news away, they become a filter, for whatever they want their boss or a Pope to know. Others act like a protective shield to handle the large input and output of information and correspondence that can give the impression concerns are being taken care of.

Where there is power there are often negative forces that will work to take control of as much of that power as possible, in the background can find cover and avoid personal attention.

Many guardians of human rights are needed to insure there are sufficient legal protections and other kinds of safeguards against the many selfish, greedy, hateful kinds of acts, that have resulted in so much misuse of others."

So hungry, having such a hard time with this fasting. Won't get my saved noon meal until after 5 pm. Couple hours from now! I'm feeling like each cell of my body is starving, crying out. So, talked myself into drinking a cup of ginger tea, after I had already had an orange earlier this afternoon, left from dinner a couple days ago.

It is so much easier to fast when in a Church or at the fountain, in St. Peter's Square praying. To always be hungry is such a drag; rarely feel that kind of hunger except when fasting like this. My oldest daughter has told me about her feelings when she tries to curb her appetite by a fasting diet, "Eventually it seems to wear you down, and you have an almost uncontrollable need to feast" and now I am experiencing that, it seems beyond my will power today.

One of the purposes for this fast is to stay in solidarity with those who, without a choice are literally starving everyday of their lives. That is much harder to do than I thought it would be. Even though I have fasted before for a special need, but not for so long a time, and having to go to the Vatican each day, is an added stress.

It seems a wonder I don't have a headache today too, as well as this cold, so hard to pray right now. How much harder it must be for those not doing a voluntary fast, which at least gives me some comfort to know it is going to end eventually, not get worse. Something like a vow of poverty when it is no longer a voluntary gift to God, poverty that becomes involuntary, is so much worse. Having a choice is important, to have that feeling of free will. Turned to Psalm 130:6

"My soul waiteth for The Lord".

Another unanswered letter:
May 2012
To Pope Benedict XVI,

As Camus once noticed:
"Official history is written by those who make history, not by those who suffer from it".

You, our present Pope, have this opportunity in our history that will really make the difference, in the lives of not only millions, but billions!

Plus, would be doing something really Saintly by ending inequality for the female half.

Without giving equal rights within the Church to women, inequality will continue to be justified in the minds of those few, who control or are now hoarding back most of the money and resources in the world, rather than using enough of the profits to pay decent wages and benefits, that causes millions to live on less than one meal in a day.

Please become the living Saint we so desperately need in our world.

A Friend "In Christ",

Betty C. Dudney

Several years later in writing this I chose to believe he has chosen to become a Saint, rather than continue to be such a

Pope.

Maybe he felt that was the only way to breath new life into our world. Who knows or can be sure how free or tied a person's hands are Or, how many knives are pointed at them, forcing them to feel they have been backed into a corner or leaving them little choice. Who is in a position to judge? Another reason why we are to leave judgment of people's motives, or holiness to God alone! As each person's situation is unique to their own!

Still can't help but wonder where one's head and heart are, if claiming to be a Catholic, and knowing it means Universal, one would not believe in the equal opportunity for the female half?

Perhaps they were taught and believe it is a male only God who created all life, with females being created as an after-thought, for a means of reproduction, and/or as their maids? It is easy to have that impression when you live all your life under only male run organizations, male centered languages and in aggressive, competitive male cultures!

Yet I have come to understand God, as a Spirit of Holy Love, who transcends any one sex or race. Who wants us, to see our humanity as one, on one small planet, living in a spirit of holy love for each other.

The Christian Jesus, a willing sacrificial Child of God had to be born a male, 2000 years ago, as females were not allowed to speak to males then without their permission or outside the immediate family, certainly not to preach in public, or even be able to go into the synagogues, or Temple, confined to an outer court for the women, slaves, foreigners. In the most conservative Synagogues, even now, they still have to sit in an outer room.

Jesus first broke that tradition by choosing a woman, a long time Disciple and one of many loyal female followers, Mary Magdalene, to be the first Apostle to announce to the others, the best of the "The Good News", the Resurrection of Jesus, that sets it apart from most other beliefs.

Part of the evidence we have of our own resurrection after this life, for an individual eternal life! Our best hope of dealing with all the fears and insecurities of living such a short time here on this earth.

Even today it continues to change individuals as well as human history once The Living God, who equally loves all, has been experienced, taking away the fears of a limited life.

Yet the female half, those who have heard God's Call in their own lives, to preach the Good News of/ as equal partners, have been blocked by most Christian sects, especially since Christianity became the official State religion, between three to four hundred AD. By the then worldwide Roman Empire.

Now many are beginning to see the female half of God's Image in a different light, coming officially from Vatican II, the last World-Wide Council of Christians, so plainly stated to put an end to the discrimination within The Church as not God's Will". *1

*1 Pastoral Constitution, Articles 29, + others, of Vatican II.

Part of the problem of discerning is it is not only God's choice as to the best time to speak to an individual, as well as to the whole, but also each one's being willing and free of sin or negative-ness to be able to hear God's Holy Spirit in their heart, which controls much of what the head can hear and comprehend.

Knowing what in scriptures are to be taken literal, or

symbolic, a parable story form or even in poetical language? About inspired words, but also about being able today to distinguish what is specifically from God and what is from the male only way of experiencing God during those times.

Today in our still sexist culture, our prejudices are incorporated into our ways of speaking and thinking, such as pronouns we use for God are male terms.
So, from childhood God is pictured in the mind, in our logic and morals as male, leaving females seemingly less than.

We have an inbred cultural sexism, not so easily changed, until one can accept that both male and female were both created in The Image of God. Verified in Scriptures from the first or Priestly Biblical version of Creation, as well as the third Creation story in Chapter 5.

As both stories state "both male and female were created in the Image of God". Quite unlike the more often repeated second creation story from another Hebrew tribal King, King Ahab I. His parable a moral tale of the influence of sin told by blaming the female other half in a patriarchal or male story form. Jewish teachers, or Rabbi's taught in parables, for this was their traditional way of teaching moral lessons.

The book of Genesis is a collection of creation stories handed down from the tribal campfires of the early Hebrews, written down on parchment scrolls. Somewhere beginning in 1000 to 500 B.C. the time King Ahab I had his parable included between the first and second Priestly versions, being one of the last books written of the Bible about 66-73 authored books finally voted on around the 1500's for a total of 73 officially voted on by The Council of Trent, as Church Canon.

There is so much about history and culture we either know little about or kept in the dark about.

Universal education a great challenge in the coming years, in both teaching learning to read and write as well as have an equal respect and concern for each other.

A SNAP Commentary

"Almost 20 years ago, a group of some 30 survivors of childhood Sexual molestation by priests and I wrote to Pope John Paul II in painstakingly and excruciating detail of our harrowing experiences of being raped and sexually assaulted as youngsters while attending a boarding school for boys operated by the Capuchin Franciscan religious order in rural Wisconsin.

The school, St. Lawrence Seminary, was one of a vast network of such Catholic seminaries across the United States. Pope John Paul II was keen to see a massive resurgence of places like St. Lawrence, in which priests raised children to become priests like themselves.

What we were hoping for from Pope John Paul II was justice. What we received instead was a certified letter from the nuncio curtly informing us that our letters and documents had been acknowledged. We never heard anything more from either him or the pope."

Part of that legacy, whose vast dimensions are still being uncovered, includes thousands of unprosecuted child molesting clerics, hundreds of thousands of child victims, and an institutional pattern and practice of concealing and transferring pedophiles.

Yet it was justice, ordinary justice that victims like myself and my abused and anguished classmates desperately pleaded for in our letter to John Paul so many years ago."

Peter Isely is on the national board of SNAP, the Survivors Network of those Abused by Priests, and a graduate of Harvard Divinity School.

Almost did not add this because it was so painful to even read. But is it any more painful than other children and adults, starving to death because of our present economic greed, or inequality by others?

There is no way to know where all the bucks lie on some of these universal problems, in some families as well as organizations, whenever someone weaker is left at the mercy of another it becomes possible.

A measure of each one's responsibility starts with becoming aware, first to our own state of inequality, or degree of selfishness that can seem to leave little time to do what we can to help others less able.

"An ounce of prevention is worth a pound of cure" Our partly Indian Grandmother use to tell us, being mostly English, while my other Grandmother was mostly Irish, but having some Scottish ancestors too. Former slaves from the South, also took some of our ancestral American last names. It has made it easier for me to identify with many races.

If we look back in our ancestry for even a few hundred years, we can know many of us are the result of several races or more.

Turning racial pride around has become my own source of pride, to consider myself as being a typical American Mongrel.

Racism, like Nationalism gives a sense of identity that too often turns towards being a way to exclude others with any cultural kinds of differences. Usually out of fear or uncertainty of whether another's ways will be a threat of some kind or the other. Good to be living in an economy that does best when the people are free to live and work where they most want to be and able to find their best opportunity.

Realizing it is going to be where our heart and concerns are, to how much we are going to be able to balance out, equalize in our own lives. Most of us cannot afford to go back to the one time nationalistic or tribal isolation, our ancestors had and knew how to use it even to knowing friends from enemies.

To avoid our worldwide disasters such as nuclear wars, we must learn how to turn enemies into friends, as much as is possible or risk widespread destruction that can take us back to being cavemen, in a desert land.

Customs or traditions that are harmful to others should never trump what we can confirm to be true from God's Holy Spirit and will be much better for us than so many of the more selfish traditions and prejudicial customs from our past.

"God's Ways are higher than man's ways". Many of men's ways, or traditions, have been evolving for the better since primitive times, such as slavery, racism and sexism, and other forms of inequality.

While those who are less evolved or have gotten caught up in addictive forms of greed and power tripping have created a gross misuse of people. Most of us do not want to have traditions that belittle others,

Most of us want to have good relationships with others and are evolved enough to not want to see another human being enslaved.

The same is true or equally applies about those trying to survive on so little of the world's wealth and resources.

We do see, in some forms of inequality within The

Church, there has been much progress, such as in racial discrimination. Before Vatican II, by tradition, only Italians were elected Pope in the Roman Catholic Church. Since Vatican II when it was finally officially considered to be a form of discrimination, we have had Pope John Paul II who came from Poland. Pope Benedict XVI from Germany, and our present Pope Francis from South America.

Racism in other ways within The Church does not seem so much of a problem as it was once was, hopefully it will not be long before sexism is not either.

A recent hopeful world-wide survey within The Church requested by Pope Francis is encouraging laity participation for the first time and will hopefully help to end other forms of discrimination.

Noticed in my own Parish from a small sample, only 10% did Not believe women should be given same roles as men in the activities and administration of the Church, and only about the same small number were against women being able to be Priest.

It also was encouraging in social justice issues, only 6% were against the question of whether "the Church has a responsibility to teach people their responsibility to protect each other from poverty and from physical harm and mental abuse".

And only 8% against "Do you think the Catholic Church has a responsibility to spend its resources helping people be able to live safely and to have adequate nutrition and healthcare?"

Other issues of Cohabitation, abortion, divorce, homosexuality there seemed more of a split, except for birth control, only 10% were against or thought it a sin, with 13% considered remarriage a sin. That is without an annulment from the Church that there was not a valid marriage to begin with.

So once again I am feeling there is nothing more

that I can do right now but to wait and see the results.
It seems like a real step forward for The Church.

We must wait, wait within the slowness of the Vatican's way of change. For me it should be a time for much more praying and fasting. Hopefully for those of you too, who are able to see for yourself the need to end discrimination, to create more "Equality".

This was just a small sample from one of our more progressive parishes in the Southland of America and may or may not be representative of many other parishes.

Now the question will be, are there enough within the Church that are aware and have not been misled? I can't help but trust that there are enough who are and evidently so does our present Pope, at least he is wanting to know what present day Catholics really are believing in.

For now, it seems like a big ray of sunshine in spite of the inequality many have been fed by the hierarchy for many generations, yet at least some, maybe many, have been listening more to a higher power and are willing, to turn away from men's traditions and often even misunderstandings of God's Words.

TEACHINGS ON LABOR, UNIONS

Excerpts from Catholic Social Teaching on LaborUnions, and Workers Rights: "In the first place, the worker must be paid a wage sufficient to support him and his family."
Quadragesimo Anno (The Fortieth Year) #71
On Reconstruction of the Social Order Pius XI, 1931

"We consider it our duty to reaffirm that the remuneration of work is not something that can be left to the laws of the market place; nor should it be a decision left to the will of the more powerful. Pope John XXIII, 1961

It must be determined in accordance with justice and equity; which means that workers must be paid a wage which allows them to live a truly human life and to fulfill their family obligations in a worthy manner." Mater et Magistra (Mother and Teacher) #7

Economic Justice for All #303 Pastoral Letter on Catholic Social Teaching and the U.S. Economy, U. S. Catholic Bishops, 1986

"The Church fully supports the right of workers to form unions or other associations to secure their rights to fair wages and working conditions. This is a specific application of the more general right to associate." "Work is in the first place "for the worker" and not the worker "for work."

Work itself can have greater or lesser objective value, but all work should be judged by the measure of dignity given to the person who carries it out."

Laborem Exercens (On Human Work) #6

It is right to struggle against an unjust economic system that does not uphold the priority of the human being over capital and land.

Centesimus Annus (The Hundredth Year) #35
John Paul II, 1986

Economic Exploitation

The poverty of many people in our world does not point just to their personal efforts but to our unequal distribution systems, and the misuse or the unfair use of most of the world's resources.

Some want to not claim any of the blame, or responsibility for the actions of themselves or others, or of our ancestors long gone. Yet everyone wants to receive as much as their ancestors have passed on to them, not only in terms of inherited wealth of physical resources, but social or cultural advantages, and do not see this as a moral contradiction.

It is our physical instinctive animal like natures to be selfish, Yet we have the capacity to be and to evolve higher, left to our free will and love of freedom.

In our highest human nature, we naturally want to treat others equally, just, and fair, if for no other reason than to be able to expect to be treated in the same way by others.

We can reach a godly, pure or holy kind of love when we have an equal concern for others, as well as ourselves, as the fullness of the universal golden rule.

Now we are at a point where we must turn our beliefs into the kind of daily actions that benefit us all. To do less is to be less.

Very much like what Desmond Tutu reminds us when he says:

"People of religion have no choice in the matter. Where there is injustice and oppression, where people are treated as if they were less than who they are-those created in the image of God—

you have no choice but to oppose . . . that injustice and oppression."

"We do our religions scant justice, we put our religions into disrepute, if we do not stand up for the truth, if we do not stand up for justice, if we are not the voice of the voiceless ones, if we are not those who stand up for those who cannot stand up for themselves."

"Ubuntu" is the African word for the essence of being human. It speaks of how my humanity is caught up and bound up inextricably with yours. We are made for togetherness, for family." "With our fellow human beings, with the rest of creation."

"We inhabit a universe that is characterized by diversity. There is room for everyone; there is room for every culture, race, language, and point of view. "Almost everywhere the rulers are out of touch with the people."

INEQUALITY BREEDS WAR

Inequality breeds our wars, mistrust, destruction, starvation, and injustices of all kinds. It can only be stopped though the practice of the universally known Golden Rule.

Inequality is the immorality of dictatorial, as well as most of our current capitalistic economics, that claims to be a "free market" but in reality plays by the similar 'laws of the Jungle', with the only thing free is a lack of morality! where the strongest may seem for a time to survive well, and the rest easily enslaved in a culture of low to moderate monthly living wages, high taxes, often with lifelong debts and obligations.

Within a moment's notice, one's economic base can be wiped out in a stroke of a pen, by someone on the ladder above or at top of the pyramid. Little safeguards in the poor countries without even basic safety nets of food or shelter.

Only about 5% with degrees, ties or special influence, are put in well paid positions as managers, or enforcement heads to keep in line about the 15-20%of the world's populations, who are paid at least living wages. This allows only a few International Corporate Head CEO's and/or Government Department Heads to be able to control the vast majority of workers. While at the top 1% keep control of over 90% of the economy

To do this CEO's are paid thousands of times more, with other perks and bonuses not available to most workers.

At the top the gross profits increases intolerance, sexism, unfairness and based on workers competition with each other rather than cooperation, with few as possible workers hired.

Some of the excessive profits are used by those on the top to buy off politicians, to prevent regulations often needed for worker or public safety. The use of social security and health insurances, to avoid large corporate taxes, so most profits are put in the hands of the larger stockholders, the 1%, whose only work is to meet yearly to be able to siphon off most of the profits with large insider contracts for war products, for military killing, damage and destruction of people, as well as to the land, sea and air.

Major stock holders, who can work both sides of many national conflicts, to make contracts with one country, than the other.

Should we not be Praying daily, as well as deciding how best to stop these and many other present dangers? For we need no more Hiroshima's, or no more Japanese kind of nuclear leaks. Before it takes 20 years for statistics to leak out to us how many millions of lives will be shorten because of their still leaking nuclear radiation.

Let's get it back, deep into the ground where it belongs. No more nuclear bombs, no more destructive nuclear reactors.

Till then, I have learned the safest thing you can do is to daily take a small amount of kelp, or seaweed, that absorbs radiation. Best now not harvested near Japan!

Can be gotten in most health food and grocery stores is sold plain or there is a seasoned kind, to me makes it tastier.

For the radiation we all are being exposed to, some more than others. Depending upon when it was swept up into the upper atmosphere and what part of the world it continues to fall upon.

While much of the radiation settled in the areas around Japan, and nearby oceans, much still goes up into the upper atmosphere and circles the Earth, within days falling where it will, on water supplies, farmland and lasting for hundreds of years!

How much more leakage will we allow? While the Present company who built those in Japan is still being given charge of stopping the leakage and estimates Another 40 years!

There is medicine that can be individual prescribed such as Potassium Iodine, but only for those severely exposed because of the dangerous side effects of too much iodine. Our bodies only make about a teaspoon a year, so easy to get too much.

For some known radiation burns, one can also use a teaspoon salt in a liter or quart of water, to be sipped on during the day. Too much salt not being good for you either. With a mostly unknown amount of exposure, a 4X4 thin wafer of seaweed, available in most health food stores, like Trader Joe's in the U.S.A. Also found here in Italy at Health Food and some grocery stores, is good to daily take, as seaweed is one of the few plants known to absorb radiation.

When or if you know you have been exposed to a lot, on returning from outside, be sure to shake off your outer clothing before entering wearing a different set of clothes inside, washing separately. Then staying inside as much as possible, especially young children and youth of childbearing age, to prevent or minimize later birth defects.

When having to be outside, best to use an umbrella, or wear wide brimmed hats. Those living near the Pacific coastlines are at present most in danger from Japans radiation fallout.

Do we really need more nuclear reactors or military spending for research to be able to kill or cause cancer more than they already have?

Revelations, in the ninth chapter from the prophecy of bitter waters was fulfilled in 1986 with the Chernobyl (meaning bitter waters) accident, now Japan's continuing nuclear leaks add to it.

Past time to insist this 12,000 years of active destructive radiation be put back deep into the ground. For that to happen we are going to need many to Act, Pray, even to fast when possible, to be able to stop more such disasters.

"THE EARTH IN MINIATURE"

Written by an anonymous Columbian Professor as we enter into the 21's Century.
He reduced the population of the earth to the size of a small village of exactly 100 people who would look very close to something like this. As a synopsis:
In this village there would be 57 Asians, 21 Europeans, and only 4 persons from the Western Hemisphere, and 8 Africans!

52 of these would be female, 48 would be male. 70 would be non-white, while the other 30 would be white or Caucasian.

Only 30 would be Christians, 70 would not be. 90% would be Heterosexuals, 10 would be Homosexuals.

Less than 5 persons out of a 100 would own or have control of most of the Village resources. Most of those 5 would be from or have strong ties to North America.

Of the total 100 people in the Village 80 would live in subhuman conditions. 70 would not be able to read. 50 or half would be suffering from malnutrition with 1 person on the verge of starvation, one other person would actually starve each day from each 100!

Can this be fully understood without some measure of moral concern for the well-being of the whole?

The Professor says:
"If you have risen this morning with good health, have enough to eat, and no disease that puts you in the process of dying, then you are much more fortunate than many who will not be able to survive much longer."

"Even more, if you are not one of those who are caught up in a war, or in violent conflict, be in jail, or have the agony of being tortured, the pain of slow starvation, if you have escaped all this, than you are much safer than most of the people in this world."

"If you have food in a refrigerator, clothes in a closet, a ceiling over your head and a place where you can sleep tonight, you are richer than 75% of the people in your world. And you are one of the most fortunate ones, if you can read this."

"So, work today as if you don't need the money, Yes, even as if you have been really hurt like most, Dance now as if nobody will be seeing you. Sing now as if nobody is listening to you!"

Thank You Professor for sharing that with us!

A COMING EQUALITARIAN AGE

If you see such inequality as a grave danger, or as a disadvantage to yourself, as well as to others, don't we need to make this a number one priority for each of us today and every day, until we can be sure equal opportunity exist for all?

Like in any war for Freedom, you must be willing to give, even sacrifice, especially at this pivotal point in history. It may be our last chance to end this inequality for so many, Not just for a better way of living, or to make a decent salary, to have good working conditions for those we need, but also there are all kinds of freedoms in this fragile world situation that can suddenly be taken away, as it has in other times, most recently piece by piece.

The solution begins in our relationships with each other, by treating each other with equal fairness, for this is where inner peace really does come from. More precious and lasting to the soul, or spirit, than all the possessions or cold physical gold we might think we could be able to accumulate, only to suddenly lose it all, such as when we lose our health.
Even possibly eternal life, when God calls for our very next breath.

In the Light of the eternal, we must all one day come face to face with, the "I AM THAT AM" The Supreme Intelligence of "LOVE ONE ANOTHER, EVEN YOUR ENEMIES", *10. Not for God's sake as The Source of Creation is a Spirit of

Love, without needs!
*10 Exodus 3:14; Luke 6:27; Matt. 22:39-40
It is for our sakes, as Children of a Loving God, so that we too, may have the best of all things!

According to present day scientific evidence, we know human beings have both female as well as male qualities, within each one, yet each created unique and unlike no other.

To evolve and better survive with each other it becomes necessary to give up intolerances such as being homophobic. It helped me when I found out in the animal kingdom, many are known scientifically to have about the same amount of gayness as humans do, around 10%!

For the past 5000 years our history has been written, interpreted, and sometimes misinterpreted by the more competitive, and aggressive males who were able to gain the reigns of controls, in the home, workplace in governments. A surprise when I found Archeological evidence of Matriarchal cultures that proceeded this last male dominated age, believed also to have lasted for about 5000 years.

In our times, after as many as 10,000 years now, of humans trying to live together in different ways and to come out of the most recent violent way of male/only rule, we have even more of a need to come into the Equalitarian age, of Equal Rights, Equal Respect, and Concern, not only for those who are like us, but for those who are not, in such a way that our rights are not intruding on others, or visa-versa.

Everything begins within ourselves, we have to balance first our own or lack of equal concern and respect for others, in our homes, work, community, before we can naturally care about others with an equal concern.

Living in such an unequal world as we have had is going to take some conscious balancing to heal, and then to share that healing. It makes sense to do so because all of us can find ourselves in some minority and will eventually have a need to rely on one another's respect and extended equal rights towards us. To live in a secure safe world.

Much of our past inequalities have been allowed to continue because of so many hierarchal power systems, as well as our natural fears of those who are different and how their ways might affect us. Both are dangers to our safety today, we are each first called to be sensitive or tolerant to where others are.

On another mental and emotional level, the violence and amount of force that has been used in the past, to continue the unequal traditions and customs that are in our economic and political systems and have been going on for so long. Many do not feel we have the ability to change it for the better? Yet a non-violent revolution, to treat others more fairly, has also been going on among many and growing gradually, especially since the time of Jesus.

One of His last deeds was to send Mary Magdalene, after His death and resurrection, to be the first Apostle to the other Apostles and his followers. The first to announce the "Good News of Resurrection, the Christian hope for into Eternal Life, after this life!

When we are willing to put a totally giving God kind of Holy Love into our heart, as Jesus said, even for your enemy's. Then

95

God's Spirit will be able to guide such a loving heart to the fullness of Truth. This is where we can recognize ourselves as equally part of the whole.

Putting us in a state of being or feeling in a New Age spiritual lingo as "In harmonics with the whole". To love and do good to an enemy, is the only chance you have to make him a friend instead of an enemy". This teaching extends our ability to love and care for others beyond just those who love us.

It is not for an accepted dogma, sect, or official organization, but for "A Way" of being Spiritually empowered, that can be found in both Eastern and Western faiths, and expressed in the Golden Rule, universally found, in most of the world's beliefs systems as well as within loving hearts, with or without belonging to a dogmatic belief or sect.

Allow others to spiritually be where they are. Without having to take on our cultural baggage, will help us to see our common humanity. For we can only have more safety and security when everyone has a security net or at least the basics necessities?

Do just a few have the right to take so much more than their share? Or do a minority have the right to prevent the chance for everyone to become the best each has the talent and interest to be? If the answer is no, then what is a higher goal, except stopping wars and nuclear disasters, stopping this present economic, sexual, and female inequality?

It will take the power of many to insist, in all kinds of ways, to create for our-selves a better reality, without hurting others.

What are some of the ways this could be done non-violently? I believe it will take many local to some worldwide Human

Rights Groups!

Could start with local groups of friends and trusted family members.

The first we tried we called the Golden Rule Family as a non-profit, of no more than 12 in each family group, and when it became larger, one or two volunteers would then break off to form another such group, the best way to grow and still keep small enough to know and trust those in your group and be equally concerned about the others as well as your own self-interest.

Groups networking with other groups, seems best to coordinate, to work towards goals for your area, state, nation, even with international goals.

As one group reaches the ideal number of 12, for personal protection as well as working best together, it is closed, till that number becomes less, or someone chooses to start, or go into another group. Hopefully putting their efforts into joining or forming a state group, depending on each one's interest of working on a local, or a National even an international group.

In this way contact is kept with groups you originally start with, but your primary efforts will be in the region where each one feels they have the most to offer and feel best working in that area.

This seems like it would be the best way for such volunteer groups to sustain interest, have the energy to go forward, and when necessary, doing possible needed fundraising for agreed on goals. There should never be member dues, for this is a people's party and the poorest of the poor should feel welcome, without taking needed funds for others. Donations from those with extra would of course always be welcomed, but as free will gifts. Reasonably priced T-Shirts, with a world design and local logo are possible items to be sold for fundraising with other possible usable items, the majority in a group have voted on. Silent auctions of volunteer talents or other such things might be added or better for some groups more than others.

To prevent the misuse of other people's funds any eventual paid staff should be limited to first being a member for at least a year, and then being voted at each yearly term, best using yes and no secret ballots. Including yearly held elections for each group, maybe a chairman, secretary and or treasure. Each for no more than their share of times elected.

We decided in our first group to have only one meeting a year required to maintain membership out of the ideal twelve-monthly meetings. Which could be done by email, telephone, or by mail, as well as actually meeting as we normally do in person.

99

AH, THE ROMANTICS OF ROME

Awaken today from the noise of two lovers quarreling several floors below my street window. Was it too much of a Saturday night party? Too much alcohol, it looks like, for both! Her tears flowing and pacing up and down as his anger increases, ebbs and starts again. He seems to be saying this is all her fault, over and over; they play a duet, back and forth.

As the sun chases the shadows away he continues to rant and rave, while off and on he checks his pockets, then searches her purse, it becomes obvious they must have lost their last euro's. Maybe they were robbed, spent too much, maybe even a pickpocket, anyway it was somehow all her fault!

The money, the very last of their money is gone. No more, just all gone!

Why does not one of them just walk away, start anew at least until another day? But maybe they have nowhere to walk away too!

They must both be in shock to just stay when there is nothing left for them here, or obviously left of their once, maybe just hours ago hot romance, now their dislike is just as strong, no love left between either of them for now.

No respect or concern for each other left. Yet marching back and forth, they both continue to rant, or he rants, and now she weeps. Both caught up in their own unseen web of consternation, frustration, anger, accusations, sorrow, and both in a continuous wringing of hands, turning to and then away from each other, then turning back again to what might have been, now away, to not even a hope left.

I could not watch the show anymore.

As even a hungry seagull started to chime in. Thank Goodness by the time I dressed, got downstairs and out the door they were gone.

At this earlier time, I would be able to escape the more usual rush to St. Peters that would soon begin, today being Sunday and a day of Blessing for Pope John Paul II, who also had promised to help the hundreds of religious, who came here for the second time, to ask for "Equality" in St. Peters Square.

He had promised them he was going to do what he could, in the memory of John Paul I, and they chose to believe him for a few more years, till he finally announced sometime in 1984, that Jesus had only chosen males to serve at the altar!

Once when Pope John Paul II was on Television, in anguish I asked God to know why he was not following Vatican II, to end such Christian discrimination. God gave me the vision of "seeing" his hands tied behind his back and a knife held over him.
I know it is to their advantage for The Church to make him a Saint; even I had felt his natural Charisma, had known and was thankful he had helped the Solidarity labor movement in Poland, when he had been a Bishop there. Yet I just can't help now these mixed emotions about him. Was he too just a victim of 5000 years of sexism and inequality?

Arriving early today in St. Peter's to share mass with just a few, maybe 12 others of the faithful, at one of the side altars.

Without chairs we stood and knelt several times on a cold

marble floor, just to be as close as possible to the altar as the host was offered in Thanksgiving, for this Christ meal.

At the sharing of peace, you could see in their faces most had been refreshed and fed for another busy day here. Except not for me today.

Walking out of St. Peters Basilica and looking over the huge piazza of St. Peters Square you could see the crowds streaming in from all directions.

The crowds continued to increase, seeming to become almost a roar till I could not hear my own inner voice, commenting on Jesus presentation at the temple. I needed to be in a quieter place so went outside the walls to walk around the quieter outer walls of Vatican City.

A long, at least hours walk, up the hill and around the high walls were there is more silence, but only able to finish the joyful mysteries.

Tried to come back into St. Peter's Square to continue but just could not finish, the crowds seemed so dense. It felt more like a carnival ground than a sacred place.

My emotions are not strong enough to deal with being here today. By noon I was back in my room wondering why I had not stayed with such a crowd of people there to witness to.

I should have, maybe if I had had more courage myself today, more belief, that it was not as hopeless, as it all seemed to me right then.

103

Today I will pray for no more nuclear reactors, or military spending, or for research aimed at killing and destroying life.

Help us Dear God to rise up as your people to live out your better guidance.

One of my goals of praying was to say the complete Rosary each day, thinking it would help center and keep me focused, as well as help me in fasting. I feel the need to be here strongly yet also so inadequate to be trying to do such a big project as to end discrimination within this Church.

The Rosary also helps me be more at ease, or more certain, in doing what I sure would prefer not to have to do.

Still wondering why God seems to pick people, such as myself to do God's Will that would rather not or is it just that no one would really want this job. But then why pick one of the least who doesn't has any worldly power? No matter, I have had to learn that God's ways do not always, make much worldly sense to most of us.

Am finding being more comfortable with witnessing does seem to correspond to saying the Rosary. Greater ease, with the completion of one Mystery to the next, it does usually seem to help give me spiritual strength! From the first "Joyful Mystery", that tells of the Annunciation to Mary, by the Angel Gabriel, then her journey to visit with her cousin Elizabeth, who too was with Child, later to be known as John The Baptist.

Elizabeth telling Mary he leaped in her womb as she greeted Mary!

The remembering of the birth of Jesus is in the Third Joyful Mystery, and in the fourth when Jesus is presented at the Temple; the final Joyful Mystery is finding Jesus, teaching in the Temple, as early as twelve years old.

The next five "Luminous Mysteries" start with the baptism of Jesus. Then as He began his public Ministry performing one of His first miracles at a wedding feast, by changing water into Wine, in spite of His seemingly reluctance, He does respond to His Mother request, that they had run out of wine, and so being an obedient Son performs His first public miracle.

The third Luminous Mystery is about Jesus preaching the Good News of God's equal Love for each one of us, sinners as well as the self-righteous. One of the reasons humility is so important, in seeking Holiness or coming from a word meaning Wholeness.

This is a way to see how we all sin daily by what we do, or fail to do, and yet each still are Loved, and are of Equal value to God!

If we are each a sinner or self-righteous, how can any of us think we are much better? Or for that matter much worse, than any other? Especially when we "walk in their shoes", as the old saying goes. Humility is partly recognizing the Equality we do share.

It is Pride that wants to put our individual selves on a pedestal, or to put others below us in inferior positions, to be able to assert our will, or sometimes it could be just to make us

feel better about ourselves, even at the expense of others.
Pride may rear its head when we are only considering self.
Then the opposite, when we ourselves have been put down too often, as not being enough and have a lack of self-worth or very little self-confidence, that makes us think others are so much better!
Another form of pride is thinking we deserve more than others, because we feel favored, or we have more in some way such as talents, good looks, money.

Still needing to see in another light that "Those given more, much more is expected from them". Best to see reality from an unselfish way, and not how we might sometimes feel like Lording it over others, or to shy away from doing what we can, when or where needed.
Selfishness and greed can make it seem justified to take more than what we need, or not want to share fairly that leads us later to the misery of wrong decisions, and actions.

Very hard to break habits of this kind of thinking we have learned, or from the way we have been treated by others, who may or may not have been able to love or care much about us. As we keep evolving, growing in knowledge and spiritual maturity, we can't help but become aware of our own "Equality". To cherish our Equal rights that stop at the Equal Rights of others.

The fourth luminous mystery is when Jesus is transfigured on the Mount of Tabor. There the Disciples Peter, John and James, found themselves on a mountaintop with Jesus, when Moses and Elijah appeared. They reported God saying from Heaven,

106

"This is my beloved Son, listen to Him".

St. Peter is said to have established the first Church as Bishop of Rome, the then Capitol of the World. He would be one of the first of many Bishops of Rome, who would become Martyrs for several hundreds of years, before it would become the state religion and persecutor of other beliefs.
Religious tolerance and freedom of beliefs are human rights that must be legally protected.

St. James, a brother or cousin of Jesus, not possible to be sure as the same word was used in those days for close family members. He would later become Bishop of the then persecuted Church in Jerusalem, known as "The Way", until he too, was Martyred, being beheaded. His Skull is enshrined in an altar of the old Armenian Monastery within the Old City.
Disciples of St. John continued his teachings in the Gospel of John, as well as three letters from St, John and in his exile on the Island of Patmos, his final writings, the last book of the Bible called Revelations, consisting of three separate visions, from Chapters1-3; 4-11; and the last vision in Chapters12-21.

These prophetic writings said by some to have been fulfilled within a few years after being written, as some were while others note parts in the book as yet to come, as is true in most Biblical Prophecies that can pertainto the present, as well as for future times.

Such as the Temple being rebuilt and a return of Jewish animal Sacrifices, after a world-wide take over by the antichrist and another disastrous war, with Jesus literally returning, to be seen by all, and even the eventual giving of a "1000" years of Peace. *11

Prophecy is to give us hope as well as to warn, For us to prevent the worse from happening, when and If we choose to heed the Prophecy..

We can wait, hope, and pray for the perfection of humankind, and most of all, actually do what we can while here, as each is able and given as ours to be a partner of Christ part of God's Hands, in some way, while here.

Jesus said we would be judged, after this life, by "what we did, or failed to do to the least here, plus what we did or failed to do would be the same as being done to him".

The 5 sorrowful mysteries tell us of Jesus sufferings, by people who act much like ourselves. Acting as a reminder of our need to do God's Will, rather than our own, especially when the flesh is weak, even to the carrying of the Cross, as Jesus did. Jesus suffering in a Roman Trial, His being beaten, carrying His Cross to Calvary, Dying on a Cross, Reaching out to the previous dead.

The Glorious Mysteries deal with the resurrection of Jesus, after three days rising from the dead, being seen by many. Jesus assured hundreds after his resurrection, appearing in person, even passing through locked doors where his disciples had gathered in fear, both in a physical real touchable form who ate with his Disciples, as well as in a showed them his Spiritual Supernatural Form.

His resurrection was what took away the fear from His Disciples who were suffering from much fear at that time, of thinking because of the death of Jesus he must had been just a physical nature and they knew the danger they were then in, just for being his followers.

Many would see him after his resurrection and be there on the Mount of Olives, to see Him as He ascended into the Heavens, completely changed their fear of death into the courage to become more Christ like.

Some of the final words Jesus gave for all those who would follow as disciples, to "Receive the Holy Spirit, who will lead you to the fullness of Truth". *14
*14 John 3:3; John 14:26; John 16:1

The last two Glorious Mysteries remind us of the two infallible Statements declared by Popes later with in the Church.

Both are about Mary being the mother of Jesus. Being pure enough to contain the Divine nature of God, and on her deathbed, recorded in Church Documents, as also seen assuming directly into Heaven, after her last breath here.

She is to be considered a Heavenly Mother to all who believe in Jesus, and given by The Church the title of "Queen of Heaven, and of the Earth".

I had not felt a calling by Mary to come here fasting and praying for "Equality", only from God. Yet once Mary did urge me, during a time in prayer, to make a pilgrimage to a Basilica dedicated to her in Mexico City, many years ago.

That became an eye opener for me, not only to be among so many poor, in worldly terms, yet also so rich in Spirit, and to see for myself the evidence of the many miracles done there, by Mary, Queen of Heaven.

Such as the miracle of her Image imprinted on his "Tilma",

that should have long ago rotted being just a fiber cloth of a poor man's coat, Juan Diego had worn when She appeared to him several times to convince his Bishop to build a Church, in Mexico City.

The miraculous Image and other Miracles would eventually cause millions of conversions to Christianity. The Aztec Indians, who had previously sacrificed humans to the gods, were many of her converts.

I believe Mary is Queen of Heaven here too, for no other reason than she was and is the Virginal, without sin, Mother of Jesus and cares in a special way for all who believe, especially those with a cross of their own to carry.

111

LAST TIME IN ROME

This was my last general audience with Pope Benedict XVI, while here in Rome. Did manage again to get close enough to the railings, when the Pope passed, to get another letter to one of the guards who walk beside and behind the Pope Mobile, he is up too high to be able to give it to him personally. I think this was the same guard who has taken it before.

Again, The Pope came by the section near where I had been last week, this time he circled two times around, the first time our eyes had meet. It was just not a very pleasant look, which I would have much preferred to see. Little doubt in my mind, that either his hands, like Pope John Paul II were according to the vision I was given, are tied or that he just does not have any intention of allowing females to have an opportunity for ordination. Either way what a shame!

Right now, that continues to keep the female half of God's nature in an unbalanced state of emotional male dependence and even in many cases slavery, as well as the male ego in a continued more aggressive state, that might have been beneficial to cavemen, but not to the times of our present-day world needing a needed feminine cooperation spirit the most, right now.

We have had and still have the chance of making this a paradise on earth for most of us; instead of the hell the majority are forced to live in. If that is what he chooses, what he may think is preserving the continuity of "The Church" but I see it as only ending up as a living Museum.

Yet I also believe Life, Liberty, and Righteousness is going to eventually prevail. I will stay with-in the Church as a remnant because God keeps telling me too, as I believe many others will to.

Reading this over a year later, I think now he did realize enough, for he has done maybe the only thing he could do, in his circumstances, retire so a new Pope would have that honeymoon length of time to create a change, for sometimes only what a change of the guard could do, in this case be able to make it better for the female half.

I can hope he does not hate me, but better if it has to be directed against me, then the message. Was able to write a few poems on my way home, so grateful just for being able to come home, to still being alive.

Thank Goodness, Praise God. May I never have to come back again, at least not to witness?

Have learned to love Rome in all its specialness, as well as the little of the similar to middle California countryside I have been able to see. Did get to go for a heavenly day, to the Hot Springs for my achy bones, an hour's ride in the country by a free special bus from the health resort there. Another time went to see, the uncorrupted body of St. Clare. At her convent close to St. Francis Monastery.

It was hard to tell much from the distance where The body can be viewed, but the bus ride and seeing the area was worth taking the day to go there.
She had been St. Francis lifelong friend, and both their Monasteries are close to each other, both so dearly loved, who gave their all for others.

IF JESUS CAME BACK AS A WOMAN

IF JESUS CAME BACK AS A WOMAN
WHERE WOULD SHE GO TO PREACH?
CERTAINLY NOT TO THE MOTHER CHURCH
FOR THAT IS CLAIMED BY MALES FOR
MALES ONLY.

PERHAPS TO A CONVENT
INSIDE CLOSED DOORS BE HEARD
THE SAME CLOSED DOORS OF THE TEMPLE
2000 YEARS AGO WHERE WOMEN WAITED
IN THE OUTER COURT AS PROPERTY

NO WONDER OUR WORLD IS IN STILL IN CHAOS
WHEN ONLY HALF OF THE WHOLE CAN
PRESUME TO RULE OVER
THE OTHER HALF!

The great thing about poetry is in the writing of it
you feel it is coming from a very special place within
your thoughts, not normally experienced, don't think
the conscious mind has much control of what comes
out. I can go over it to try to smooth it a little, but
the essence just comes out as it wills. Way beyond
me how! Think this one was a bit longer at one time but can
only remember this much of it now.

MESSAGE TO POPE FRANCIS

July 1, 2013
Our Holy Father Francis,

Am Writing forty years after being given the Prophetic Word of "EQUALITY" by God's Holy Spirit.

Have witnessing to, as well as at the Vatican, since 1985. Three times to three Popes, for the ending of our inequality, discrimination, especially for the female half of God's Image. Without ending inequality within the largest of our Christian institutions, how can we expect it to be ended elsewhere in our world?

Till then half of our world must live on daily wages of about U.S.$3.00. Today 25,000 children will continue to starve to death, millions more will go to bed hungry tonight.

Not to mention 7 out of 10 children will be unable to go to school to learn even to read or write because they must go to work, as young as 5-6 years old.
90% of our world's economy and resources are in the hands and control of less than 2% controllers. Resources and Labor, God means to be used for the benefit of all.

I believe you are close to God's Holy Spirit, and will help to lead our world out of the inequality and the evils of sexism and racial discrimination, and not continue them, as the Church has for so long, at such a cost. A Friend "In Christ",
Betty C. Dudney
www.goldenrulefamily.org

FORM EVOLVING RELATIONSHIPS

116

Heard an excellent homily here in Nashville this morning from a Black Priest, who had been in Uganda at the time of 9/11, ten years ago.

He was speaking on today's Gospel message of Jesus teaching on forgiveness! When Peter offered to forgive 7x7, thinking that was most generous, from his culture of an "eye for an eye", and where many of us seem to still be in!
But Jesus said no matter how good and forgiving we think we are, we need to forgive at least ten times more! *12 Matthew
*Matthew:18:21,22

This Priest mentioned, how shocked he and his people were, that such a thing as 9/11 could happen, the destruction of so many lives, from such an act of violence.

Now ten years later, what a difference it would have made if we had acted as a Christian nation by giving our enemies and the world a great moral lesson, instead of acting in violence.

By doing the wiser and better thing of forgiving. How many more lives would NOT have been lost in the wars since, and still continues, from our "getting even" that have only made us even more like the dreaded Roman Empire of Jesus time.

Many now live fearfully, because of all this violence and destruction, from America reacting negatively to their own East/West political policies, which is what terrorist claim and most likely did help to cause revengeful actions of 9/11.

Forgiveness and seeking understanding and reconciliation for such hatred would have been the Godly way.

This homily stirred my thoughts to see more clearly how we

have been outsmarted by a spirit of evil. What a safer place this world would be for us as Americans now, who in the past have been so admired and looked up too, in most parts of the world, but now we are in constant danger in whatever country, even in our own, because of one more revengeful response.

Plus because of this widespread retaliation and fear, we have also lost most of our once cherished privacy freedoms, with the early after 9/11 passage of the Patriot Act, taking away freedoms that once made our country envied, by people throughout the world!

So much of our National Taxes, an admitted 40% that we publicly know of, have been going to support an over bloated military.

We have the most military/industrial complex any nation has ever had, even though we were warned of this danger many years ago, from former President Eisenhower, as he left the office.

Do we have time to insist on a better "Way"?
Is there time left to revitalize our Freedom Loving nation in the art of Loving One Another, even our enemies? The value to us, as well as others of forgiveness, if for no other reason than to have the hope of a longer life while here on this earthly plain, and possibly eternal life?

Do we have a responsibility for the health, safety, and prosperity in the rest of our world?

It seems past the time to commit our personal actions, and our government to be the best it and we can be.

Here we find ourselves on this planet Earth, traveling through space, with billions of other human beings and many national governments, some of which have waged wars resulting in the deaths of multi-millions of people and uncountable injuries, with no end in sight.

Wars to a great extent, we can attribute to a relatively small number self-serving "controllers", manipulators and other power seekers, compared to most of us who for the most part favor peace and Goodwill.

Are we willing to put our necks out as far as are our hearts or will we let them slowly rot and hardened into the soil from which they are formed?

Many who seek a people's balance of political power believe it can be achieved through the creation of public Co-Operatives. Local economic and political groups owned democratically and elected by the people, for the people, and not just for the profits of a few to control.

Those who oppose war and looting, need to understand a major economic interest by the largest International Corporations come from making profits off of war plus contracts with national competing war machines. So long as people hold the tribal notion that the young are sacrificial fodder for war, that a few % of men have the right to rule others by force, instead of laws by mutual consent, there can be little peace within, among nations, or world-wide.

Free people with good paying jobs and decent housing have little incentive to steal from others, nothing to gain from war and a great deal to lose. Economically, wars cost money and in a free and fair economy, the economic interests of all are on the side of peace.

War is only in the interest of those who make the profits from selling the means of destruction and pitting one group unfairly against another. We all end up being their victims. Those who make these profits are concentrated in a few International Corporate pyramids of wealth and power, only 1-2% of all of us!

Is gold (mammon) really more important than people?
People live best by protecting the equal rights of all.
Are there enough of those willing to join others in using their non-violent power for good?

It is my prayer many will join in helping where-ever the need is seen. Could have your own website, anyway best for you to work together as much as possible.

Maybe each month we could have suggestions and a vote on projects most see as highest priority. No dues, no pressure, just between you and your own Golden Rule Family.

You will need to ask God's Holy Spirit to guide you, to know where your help is most needed, or an opposing spiritual force will surely attempt to use you. Depending much on where your heart really is?
Jesus Promised, whatever you give with a Loving Heart, will be returned to you 100-fold, in this life, as well as in the next.
It has been my experience this is true even in this life and in the lives of many giving people, in one-way or another, I have known it to be so.

Love is a feeling as well as reasoning Love is equally a way of thinking, speaking and acting, and comes originally from the feeling we have been loved, because we have been.

Ideally in our maturity we realize sooner or later, a God of Holy Love, loves us, usually only after some other human in our life, hopefully a parent or caretaker, has given and also shown us their love.

Children even adults, without that "knowing" of love, seldom thrive and can even die or have little desire whether they live or die. Choosing to Love, repeats the Miracle of "Loving One Another". Love from either human love, or God's Love, that has come at the least, though the giving to us our very breath of life.

What a responsibility we have to pass on, the loving of others that requires first, a feeling of having been loved, as we learn from others who have loved us. We are reflections of that love so experienced.

POEM TO SELAH

WE LIVE OUR LIVES ALONE!
GOD HELP BE MY GUIDE
WHEN EVER I'M NOT SURE
FOR THIS I PRAY

TO LIVE THE FULLEST EACH AND EVERY DAY!
HELP ME STAY POSITIVE
IN MY WORDS AND DEEDS

ALWAYS BE KIND, HELPING OTHERS IN NEEDS
PROTECT AND SHIELD ME
FROM DANGER AND HATE

FOR MY HEALTH I HUMBLY PRAY

YES, I LIVE ALONE, YET HAVE NO FEARS

SENSING YOUR PRESENCE EVER NEAR

SELAH-AMEN

123

FORMING EVOLUTING RELATIONSHIPS

Some of our relationships are based on "I'll comfort you, if you'll comfort me" and all kinds of relationships in-between.

Doubt many of us try to build relationships, with the conscious purpose in our minds, of helping each other to grow towards an evolutionary better way of thinking.

Just to stretch our minds, to see beyond our own unconscious egos, just because our world needs us to do that right now! What are some of the ways we could evolve into? better people?

One of the first things I needed to do was not to take what others said too personally, except when you know it is being said lovingly and just to help you grow, for criticisms often come just from someone else's fragile ego or even sometimes ignorance. Such kind of ego problems you don't want to take on too.

Better to take anything negatively said as not personally meant, especially if it is hurtful, so you will be able to hear where they are really coming from.

Belonging to groups that interest you can stimulate growth in the mind, or you may choose to deaden your ability to think for yourself, such as watching too much TV.

Can you think of other choices we might make in becoming the most we can be, with some of our free time?

I've always loved to read real life stories, it seemed possible to live in a few hours, what it might have taken someone a whole lifetime to learn!

"In volumes I of "The Diary of Anais Nin" in 1966, one of her biggest struggles was to reconcile the conflict between her definitions of love as a female principle, and her work in writing that in her time, was seen as an exclusive male activity, or considered an aggressive act, especially for a woman.

When she sought help with it from a Doctor, He told her that when a neurotic woman was cured, she became a woman, when a man was cured, he became an artist!

Her Diary became a place where she could escape these definitions and let the real person she was come through.

When Freud was asked what the normal person should be able to do, he replied "to love and to work". As well as "From a healthy fusion of these two great human capacities will come power, not in the traditional sense of the word as control over others, but rather power as Energy, emanating from the individual, a source of inner renewal that generates outward and returns to the individual."

Florida Scott Maxell Shared:

"Traditional cultural imbalance between work and love, where women have been or are allowed authority only in the sphere of home, while men attend to the work of the world. Such an imbalance results in a warped expression of the individual's potential energy. For women: Self-pity, masochism, manipulation, and celebration of the torments of the heart, invalidism, and madness.

For men: slavery, war, corporate profits, destruction of the earth." . . . "The pioneers of the next advance will be dealing with the mind as a whole (Holistic). The calling or function, of each one's energy, that comes from a balanced life . . . it is scarcely news that women have suffered from much injustice throughout history, that if life has never been easy for most of the human race, it has always been very hard to be a woman, to earn a living, to maintain self-respect.

As we continue to speak more openly to each other and women to men, breaking a long silence about what a woman's inner life is like, both sexes will face freer choices in the way they will love and work."

In the Beginnings God says, "Let there be light".
Ancient wisdom says that light is the energy of the Universe, it forms existence. Present day Quantum Theory says that matter originates from light!
In The Beginnings . . .

Can there be people on other planets who are more advanced than we are, who have been here before? Some could have come to help, or some even to take advantage?

To those who have pondered the billions of stars at night, the answer seems yes, there are surely enough similar planets to our own to be able to support life.
Other supernatural beings would not have to be limited by matter as much as we humans are, in our present form. Some could be very similar to humans, or they could take on a myriad of different forms. Historically they have been reported in different ways, by different cultures.
Neither can we dismiss the ability of our mind's imaginations, or projections of fears, as well as dreams.

People who have never seen anything extraordinary will be natural doubtful, as those who have seen may be just as convinced of the reality of what has been seen.

The fruits of such encounters can be judged, as whether they are harmful or helpful, good or bad, not just to an individual but also to the whole.

This may or may not be judged in one generation correctly, often in the past it has not been. There are still more questions than answers.

"No one can See God", or we are told we see in part, and maybe only according to our own mind's Spiritual limitations.

Mark Anthony has one of the better books to most simply explain in his recent book "Afterlife Frequency" our eternal life of our own soul energy being eternal in the afterlife, how our physical finite minds being just the host of our souls eternal, personal energy within the mind, on the atomic level, beyond the physical limited life of the material. Our Spiritual Conscious souls.

Paintings and other forms of art are often set in the cultural time they were created in, with the clothes and racial features of the cultures of those times. Down through history people have seen what they believed to be visitors from "The Skies", or from other planets.

The intricate order, design, and intelligence we see in most living beings and our world, also gives us evidence of an intelligent Creator, we best not try to limit, with as little as we know beyond each one's individual faiths. With each concluding

127

in some eternal energy kind of spiritual reality.

Faith being that which we accept, but that may or may not be rooted in the experience or belief of many others.
The culture we are raised in will for the most part determines our faith and what seems most real to us. While God is said to have spoken with the lowly, as well as to those in high places! It has rarely been a physical verbal communication.

In my case, only the word "Equality" was given to share.

Most of the time for most people I've talked to, read or heard about, and for myself too, there is at most a felt spiritual communication not from actual heard words but mostly from the heart, dependent on more of where one's heart and motives are, as well as the specific purpose in God's plan for one's life. Most of the time we are left free to live our lives as we so choose. Even when we realize we have a "Calling", it is stil left with few exceptions, ultimately to our own free will choice to act on that calling. As in my case it was only as the need was specifically seen or perceived for myself that I chose to act.

Such an exception happened to me, when for me to get well after a serious laboratory work accident that almost fatally destroyed my immune system, I asked for several years for God to let me go to live in Hawaii for just even six months, thinking if anything could help me get well, being there could as it had been my dream to visit such a place for a long time, at least once in my lifetime. Everything worked out for me to be able to get a hard-to-find good job in Honolulu, this most traveled Island and my health did improve I loved it, job and all, as did my two girls and one of their friends who went with us, after I was able to settle there and had a baby sitter, as I chose to work what I had for years, the night shift.

After six months my health had much improve, at least I had been able to keep my job which before I had not been able to work more than a month or two without my immune system breaking down again. So happy, where we there, no way did I want to come back.

Yet after the six months I had asked for, after my sleep I awoke to God's recognized voice in my mind telling me it was "time to go back to California". Each day for almost a month I argued to "Please find someone else to do what-ever it was God could possibly want me to do there", for I really felt I had done my share in things like civil rights, helping to set up a health clinic for farm workers and helping to start a Peace Vigil to help end the war in Viet Nan. It seemed like I had done enough and time for someone else to do their share!

For a couple of days after the month God's voice stopped happening, and felt I had finally won this daily discussion, or argumentative on my part, that I had been having with God each morning. Until all three of the girls suddenly decided they no longer wanted to stay in Hawaii by saying they missed their relatives and friends in California, where we had lived before coming here!

Thinking they too had heard God's voice I asked them "why? All of you love it here like I do, what changed your mind?", "we don't know" they all three responded we just don't want to be here anymore. So somehow God had planted the thought to leave into their minds, I knew then it must be very important Or God to be so insistent for me to come back, for me, not for God for nothing is impossible for God, someone else could have been found, and unless we have made such a vow to give our lives over to the care of God, which I had already done a few years after seeing God's Hand, normally I think, many are pretty much left on their own Free Will.

Sometimes when we specifically ask for help and what we get is not necessarily what we have asked for, but what is known by God alone, at the time, eventually we may find out the reason but all the time you can count on it being something better for you, or those you love, always better for our souls in the long run.

Which is another area where it is not wise to prejudge and why we are asked to walk in faith. Eventually as in many things the reasons would only become apparent why much later. That not understanding the why things happen at the time, has made me feel deserted and angry with God for not always protecting myself, or others I loved who I knew to be good when disasters and losses happen.

This age-old question of why good people must suffer even sometimes seemingly more than others? Some of my ignorance came from well-meaning but not very mature spiritual teachers mostly from Sunday Schools, who often taught us if you were good, God would take care of you, kind of like a Santa Claus for good little girls and boys, but that is sometimes the opposite of what Christians or other religious good people, even children experience, that doesn't seem fair at all. Sickness certainly happens to good people, as well as bad, people can be mean, or bully misuse a child or there are numerous accidents that good people are not saved from, any more than one who is full of sin. For in the course of living our lives God does allow "Rain as well as the sun to shine on the good, as well as the bad".

Why, you may not know for years, or maybe not even in this lifetime, the most you can expect is to ask God for help to endure if not to understand, which for many reasons you are not to know for God's reasons, that would not at the time make sense, even if you were told.

Help may be asked for, and enough strength to carry you, but don't expect to be miraculous spared. When a miracle does happen, you can be assured that it is for a specific part or purpose of God's over-all plan, not specifically, rarely if ever just for you personally, that would put you in an advantage over others, but God allows for some special reason, and needs to be paid special attention to in asking at least for strength to accept, as that will be freely given. Eventually God's better plan for you or another will also be revealed, but not usually in our wanted or even needed time. It may be part of your test of faith or to eventually reveal something you could not know on your own, at the time.

Miracles are few and far between, as a rule. In other words, if you're playing a sport, and pray to win, better to pray for the strength just to finish. Why would a God who is "not a god of partiality" favor you over someone else's honest efforts? For a miracle is a rare, not a natural thing to have happen and seems to be given only for a special purpose at a special time.

The only people I've ever known or heard of, who consistently have had seemingly many miracles, where Mother Teresa's Sisters, where I had the privilege of working with some of them half a day as a volunteer seamstress in 1986, during my three months in Rome, witnessing to John Paul II to end our discrimination. Any need they had they would often pray for and many times during the time I was there, I could see that them receive not less than, or more than, but often just exactly what they had prayed for!

To them it was their normal way of living, a rare phenomenon among other religious people I have known or talked to.

My faith has remained strong for our present Pope because of His taking the name of St. Frances, another one of the few in history who seemed to have a knack of receiving many miracles or having the ear of God.

For most of us, most of the time, it is much easier to hear, and to understand, or talk to God's Holy Spirit, when you are free from any negative influences in your life that might have made you feel unworthy or the opposite of not feeling a need, or desire.

I feel very fortunate to have had few negative influences in my life and raised in a very loving, safe, and secure family with many God loving relatives during one of the better times in American history, for most of my generation growing up especially after the second world war.

It sometimes seems difficult to speak meaningfully to those who have had little experience of a safe, loving family, yet we need to trust the truth we might sense in others, to be able to understand better. Opening our minds to hear each other, and not let fears close our hearts from "seeing".

Awe of God is normal as is fear and have had to learn is not from God. Fear is from something or someone, attempting to use and control us. God created us with our own Free Will and seems to expect us to use it, as a way to mature mentally as well as spiritually.

We may think culturally in very different ways, and sometimes in very opposite ways, yet still we need have no problem in accepting or communicating with each other, if we are honest in a loving way and don't take things too personal or assume some negative without discernment or confirmation from God. Then even under trying times can stay fairly well headed, emotionally balanced.

Usually, we tend to shy away from people who don't see things the way we do, yet if we want to grow in wisdom, we must do our best to try to understand what others are saying or feeling. To be able to see things the same way we need to agree it is always better to go towards the best than the worse, then to try to understand what that might mean to each one involved, or to practice tolerance, patience.

Sometimes our dilemma is often one of "The Head verses The Heart". Needing to keep a balance between the left side, of the brain's way of thinking and the other right side of the brain's feelings, or which-ever the less felt side. Males tend to think more on their left logical side of their brain, and Females more from their feelings. One reason we are complementary and need to work together as equal partners not thinking one is being better than the other.

One tends to be more logical but self-centered the other from the heart, more other centered. Not good to be out of balance with either side. Both are good, but can be damaging if not in harmony and balance within each one as well as in reacting with others, who might be coming from a different place or space.

We need this balanced way of thinking, in the home, work

and in politics, in all our beliefs and morality. People historically have been very slow to change consciously what they have been unconsciously impressed with in their life, yet our present everyday circumstances involve life or death decisions for so many others, up to millions even billions of people, who if to survive much longer have a need for a radical change in our attitudes in areas such as in the "Equality" of equal rights, and concern for each other by ending discriminations.

I see the world's consciousness trying to make that leap and many of them realizing the need, but I also see the powers that be, like the Pharaohs of old refusing to budge. (Written before the actions our new Pope who is taking giant steps right now to make things better, don't forget to pray for him daily, as well as for all of us, as we transcend into the possibility of a better life for all.)

The primary reason I feel I had to be personally involved, is from God's Call and my life-long guidance. This is the Biblical God who has traditionally chosen the "nobody's" to confound those in power.

God chose to show me God's Hand, when I was only five years old, a birthday present, one of God's kind, who must have an ironic sense of humor, I hope someday to be more fully appreciate.

Over 200 times God's Hand is mentioned in Scriptures, as the point where God intervenes, through one of his people.

I've never seen that Hand again, not really scary looking, but by far the most powerful thing I have ever seen but did feel it in my own hand one more time about 40 years later, when after about five years in becoming a Catholic, I really wanted to leave while walking towards the Church one morning and turned back to walk towards the beach, only got about half a block when I felt God's Hand in mine. Then Spinning me back around in my tracks, so I knew I was to stay within The Church to do what I could, to witness.

It seems time to consider the many years of little personal success in trying to convince those in positions of power that "Equality" is a Divine Message to treat all with their Equal Rights in Equal Opportunity, to end injustice and discrimination against for the female half of God's Image within The Church. To make sure All children have a safety net of enough food to eat, a chance to grow to be the best they can be. It seems to me, with only a few exceptions of those in great power, that most people recognize our need to end inequality and do try to treat others with equal fairness in daily lives.

Christians know from hearing the Gospels of Jesus, to "love One Another" "even your enemies" and what is known in most other beliefs as the Golden Rule of treating others with equal fairness.

Even Satanist have managed their own twist of "do to others as they have done to you" which usually means to them to be in a mean or revengeful way as they may have been treated. Much negative behavior is in actuality a reenactment from our own past negative experiences with cruel or uncaring others, often since childhood.

Prophecy says evil still has "an allotted time" on this planet, sitting in positions of power. The more people avoid, doing anything to make things better out of fear of being noticed or singled out, the more evil is able to control, by using the fear factor that "we can get you" or a threat of what has been done to others with the bully mentality. A fear of violence held over people's heads.

When even a small minority, are willing to get together and stand up for what is right or best, many of these towers of evil have in the past come crashing down. Then we have a chance to replace them with a non-threatening support and for the better ways they are destined someday to become, if not in our near future for sure in time. What we do may not always work but it most always lessens the power of evil for our times and those who will come after us.

The golden rule is the only universal message that can be found in all the creeds and dogmas of morality that tend to divide us into separate religious sects, but mostly just different in cultural traditions or customs, but deep down most people's beliefs are for the good.

There are those in positions of power who will see any form of equality as a threat to their control, a loss of power that affects them personally. Some seem to be incapable of any real empathy or remorse. They may be suffering from a hardened heart, or even have a spirit of evil in control of them. Regardless in most of us there seems to be this natural resistance to change, even for the better! For at first change usually just does not feel as comfortable for us as something we are more use to most of the time.

What rings truest right now is to get enough people to realize, know, to see the dangers of the inequality that we are living in, not only to our own spirit or soul, but also for so many others, physically, emotionally, as well as spiritually.

It is for a very good reason one of the first of the Ten Commandments is not to make a "graven Image", that is a material or limiting human Image of God. By continuing to use patriarchal language, of speaking of God in just male terms, the Church has been the biggest promoter of this false male Image or "Idolatry".

We need to see each of us, male and female, as created in the Image of God. This is and has been my witnessing, not from just my saying it, but from God's Spirit telling me, in a mostly small quiet voice within my heart, not at all like a human voice, on very rare occasions can be an actual audible sound, as when I heard "EQUALITY" at my spiritual "rebirth".

You may need to confirm for yourself, if you have, or are willing to have, a relationship with The Living God.

"God who is Love, and when we Love we live in God, and God lives in us."   I John 4:16.

When the evils of inequality and injustice are overcome and laws to prevent them from happening again are in place, then we will be able enter heaven here, as well as there, an age of peace and prosperity for all.

Will you commit yourself to become a part of that Heaven here in the now, plus the hope of an afterlife Consciousness?

Made in the USA
Columbia, SC
21 May 2023

16463402R00076